# Greece

# Greece

BY ANN HEINRICHS

*Enchantment of the World*™
*Second Series*

## Children's Press®

*An Imprint of Scholastic Inc.*

NEW YORK   TORONTO   LONDON   AUCKLAND   SYDNEY
MEXICO CITY   NEW DELHI   HONG KONG
DANBURY, CONNECTICUT

**Frontispiece:** Flowers on Santorini

*Consultant:* Demetrios Liappas, Director, The Basil P. Caloyeras Center for Modern Greek Studies, Loyola Marymount University, Los Angeles, CA

*Please note: All statistics are as up-to-date as possible at the time of publication.*

Book production by The Design Lab

Library of Congress Cataloging-in-Publication Data
Heinrichs, Ann.
  Greece/by Ann Heinrichs.
      p. cm.—(Enchantment of the world. Second series)
  Includes bibliographical references and index.
  ISBN: 978-0-531-27543-6 (lib. bdg.)
  1. Greece—Juvenile literature. I. Title.
  DF717.H38 2012
  949.5—dc23                    2012000519

1 2 3 4 5 6 7 8 9 10 R 22 21 20 19 18 17 16 15 14 13

# Greece

# Contents

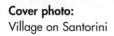

**Cover photo:**
Village on Santorini

Delphi

Loggerhead turtle

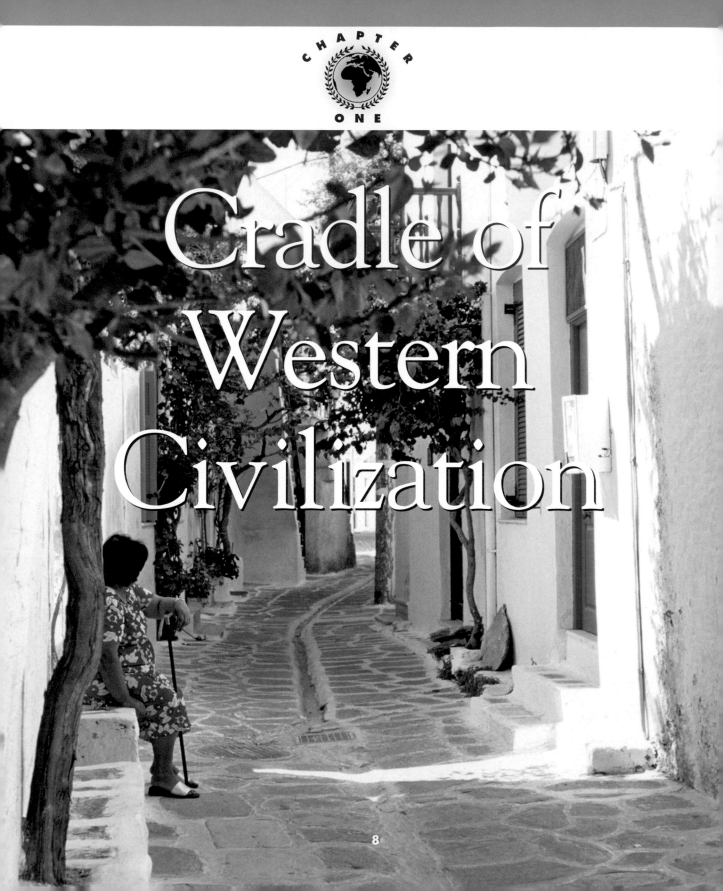

# Cradle of Western Civilization

DIMITRIS DELIVERS A POWERFUL KICK, AND THE ball zooms through the stone archway his friend Nikos is guarding. Goal! His exhausted teammates break into cheers. They won, 3–2! Dimitris and his friends love to get together on the cobblestone streets for a game of football, or what is called soccer in the United States and Canada. But playtime is over for now. Swelling with pride for his winning goal, Dimitris doesn't mind that it's time to get to work.

He glances up the steep hillside at the rows of white buildings with red-tiled roofs. One of them houses the family's cheese-making business, where Dimitris helps out. He scrambles up the narrow stone steps, two at a time—up, up, up. Soon he can smell the aroma of *formaela*, the village's traditional cheese. Inside, he stirs the hot vat of sheep's milk as it separates into curds and whey. Then he mashes the curds into tube-shaped wicker baskets.

*Opposite:* **Narrow alleys cut between the whitewashed houses in many Greek towns.**

## GREECE

- • Cities of more than 40,000 people
- ○ Other cities
- ⊙ National capital
- ∴ Archaeological site

| 0 | 100 miles |
| 0 | 150 kilometers |

ALBANIA

REPUBLIC OF MACEDONIA

BULGARIA

Pella
Kilkis
Sérrai
Kavála
Xánthi
Soufli
Philippi
Kastoria
Ptolemaïs
Alexandroúpoli
Thessaloníki
Thasos
Samothrace

Meteora Monasteries
Aliákmon R.
Mt. Olympus
Mt. Athos

Corfu
Corfu
Ioánnina
Pineiós R.
Mt. Ossa
Limnos
Paxos
Lárissa
Vólos
NORTHERN SPORADES
TURKEY

Leukas
Karditsa
Mt. Pelion
Lésbos

Delphi
Euboea
Kefallinia
(Mt. Parnassus)
Skyros
Chios
Mesolóngion
Ithaca
Thebes
Khalkis
Andros

Patras
G. of Corinth
IONIAN ISLANDS
Corinth
Athens
Tinos
Sámos
Zákynthos
Olympia
Mycenae
Piraeus
Mýkonos

Kalamáta
Náfplio
Epidaurus
CYCLADES ISLANDS
Sparta
Páros
Náxos
Pátmos
Kálymnos

Ionian Sea
Milos
Kos
Kithira
Santoríni
Rhodes
Rhodes

Sea of Crete
Khaniá
Kárpathos
DODECANESE ISLANDS
Crete
Iráklion
Knossos

Aegean Sea

Greece

Mediterranean Sea

N
W E
S

Dimitris lives in the village of Arachova, at the foot of Greece's Mount Parnassus. In ancient Greek mythology, Parnassus was sacred to the god Apollo. Not far away is the ancient site of Delphi. Here, the Delphic oracle foretold the fortunes of the powerful. Tourists on their way to Delphi used to buy the family's cheese. But now, most customers are on their way to the ski slopes of Mount Parnassus.

After his work is done, Dimitris wanders up into the rocky hillside, where wild hares are nibbling grass among the prickly pears and gray-green stones. From his favorite perch, he gazes across a landscape steeped in legends. To him, the superheroes he sees in movies are not nearly as exciting as the ancient Greek gods and warriors.

Recent traditions mean more to Dimitris than ancient legends, though. He can hardly wait for the village's annual Panigyri festival in April. It honors St. George, the patron

About four thousand people live in Arachova.

saint of Arachova and of shepherds. It also celebrates the Battle of Arachova in 1826, when Greeks won a fierce fight in their war for independence.

Dimitris will help his family put a new coat of whitewash on their house for the occasion. Everyone will drape Greek flags around the village and dress in traditional costumes for the parades and folk dances. Dimitris wonders if his grandfather will take part in the elderly men's footrace up to the domed Church of St. George. The hearty old man won the race the year before, taking home the prize lamb that shepherds brought down from a mountainside pasture.

Dimitris is very much a part of the modern age. Like kids around the world, he enjoys watching TV, listening to music, playing video games, and chatting on his phone. At the same

**An image of St. George is carried through the streets of Arachova.**

time, history and tradition are part of his life. He's proud to be Greek and proud to celebrate Greece's glorious past.

For centuries, people around the world have shared Dimitris's sense of wonder at the history, culture, and traditions of Greece. Greek legends—both real and fictional—still spark the imagination and shape the world today. Greek mythology introduced heroes such as Hercules and villains such as the Minotaur. Ancient Greeks also provided ideal models for art, science, sports, logical thinking, government, and democracy itself. This is why Greece is often called the birthplace of Western civilization.

Some travelers come to Greece to enjoy the sunny weather or the fantastic scenery. Others come to stand in awe before the ruins of ancient worlds. Either way, no one leaves without memories to last a lifetime.

**Every year, a million people visit Delphi, where the god Apollo is said to have killed a dragon named Python.**

# From Mountain to Sea

GAZE DOWN ON GREECE FROM THE AIR, AND IT might seem like a jumble of stones piled alongside the sea. How did this rocky, mountainous land come to be? One explanation comes from an ancient Greek legend. It says that when God created the world, he sifted all the earth's soil through a strainer. After every country had enough good soil, he tossed the rocks left in the strainer over his shoulder—and that became Greece!

The scientific explanation is a bit different. Scientists say that Greece was once completely undersea. It was a mass of rock at the edge of a tectonic plate—a shifting section of the earth's outer layer. That plate smashed into the rest of Europe long ago, creating Greece's high mountain ranges. Now gulfs and bays cut deeply into Greece's jagged coast. Its thousands of islands are the tips of mountains rising up from the ocean floor.

Located in southeastern Europe, Greece juts out into the Mediterranean Sea at the tip of Europe's Balkan Peninsula. Albania sits to the northwest of Greece and Bulgaria and

*Opposite:* **Craggy rocks rise from the water along the coast of Corfu, the second-largest island in the Ionian Sea.**

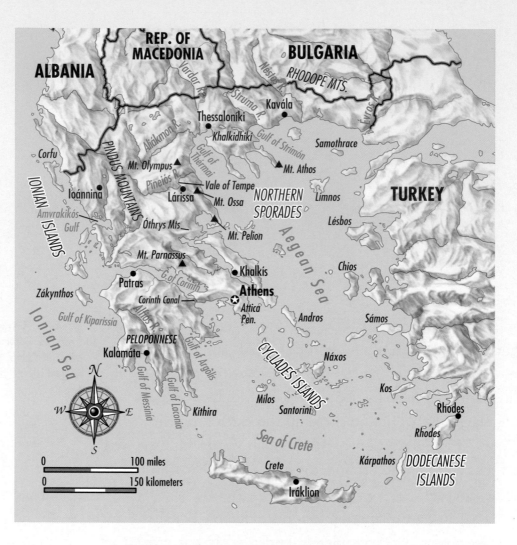

## Greece's Geographic Features

**Area:** 50,942 square miles (131,940 sq km)

**Highest Elevation:** Mount Olympus, 9,570 feet (2,917 m) above sea level

**Lowest Elevation:** Sea level along the coast

**Number of Islands:** About 6,000; 227 are populated

**Largest Island:** Crete, 3,219 square miles (8,337 sq km)

**Length of Coastline:** 9,333 miles (15,020 km), including the coasts of islands

**Greatest Mainland Distance, North to South:** 365 miles (587 km)

**Greatest Mainland Distance, East to West:** 345 miles (555 km)

**Highest Recorded Temperature:** 118°F (48°C) in Athens on July 10, 1977

**Lowest Recorded Temperature:** −18°F (−27.8°C) at Ptolemaïs on January 27, 1963

the Republic of Macedonia to the north. East of Greece is Turkey. Water encircles most of the country. Two arms of the Mediterranean Sea nearly surround Greece: the Ionian Sea lies to the west and the Aegean Sea to the east. In area, Greece covers about the same land area as the U.S. state of Louisiana.

## Mountains, Hills, and Rivers

Mountains and hills cover about four-fifths of Greece. The major mountain range is the heavily forested Pindus Mountains. This range runs down the mainland like a backbone from northwest to southeast, dividing the country in two. In the north, the Rhodope Mountains separate Greece from Bulgaria. Many of Greece's forestlands are protected as national parks.

Dramatic sandstone pinnacles rise from the plains at the edge of the Pindus Mountains.

**Regions**

Greece's longest river is the Aliákmon. It runs from the Albanian border through the Pindus Mountains of northern Greece, emptying into the Aegean Sea. Many smaller rivers cascade through Greece's valleys and plains. No large ships can navigate these rivers, though. They are too shallow, and their water levels drop in the summer heat.

## The North

Epirus is the northwest region of Greece. The Ionian Sea washes Epirus's western shores, and just to the north is Albania. Epirus is mountainous, and few people live there. Farmers graze sheep and goats on the mountainsides. Sheep's wool is important to Epirus's economy, and the region provides much of Greece's meat supply. Epirus is also known for its dairy products.

Macedonia, east of Epirus, is Greece's richest farming area. Its two broad plains—Thessaloníki and Sérrai—produce wheat, corn, cotton, tobacco, and rice. Thessaloníki, the capital of the region of Central Macedonia, is Greece's second-largest city and an industrial center. Philippi, in southeastern Macedonia, is an important historical and archaeological site, where a major battle took place during the days of the Roman

Empire. Mount Athos rises from a peninsula in southeastern Macedonia. It's the site of a group of twenty Greek Orthodox monasteries.

Thrace is the far-northeastern part of Greece. To the east, the Évros River forms Thrace's border with Turkey, and many

**Sunflowers bloom on the Thessaloníki Plain, one of Greece's greatest farming areas.**

Thracians speak Turkish and are Muslims, followers of the religion of Islam. Rising across the countryside are minarets, towers connected to mosques, which are Muslim houses of worship. Tobacco, grains, and cotton grow on Thrace's hills and plains. The silk industry once flourished in the town of Souflí, which now has several silk museums.

## The Central Hills and Plains

Thessaly, a fertile plain in the middle of Greece, was known as Aeolia in ancient times. It is encircled by the high peaks of Mounts Olympus, Pelion, and Ossa, and the Óthrys and Pindus ranges. Mount Olympus, the nation's highest point, rises to 9,570 feet (2,917 meters). According to Greek mythology, the twelve Olympian gods lived atop this mountain. Today, Thessaly is a rich farming region. Wheat, nuts, cattle, and sheep are all grown there. Lárissa and the seaport of Vólos are the region's major cities.

### Philippi

Philippi, in northern Greece, was named for King Philip II of Macedonia (382–336 BCE). After taking the city in 356 BCE, Philip named it after himself and fortified the town. Over the next twenty years, he conquered all of Greece and united the Greek city-states into the League of Corinth. After Philip was assassinated by one of his bodyguards, his son Alexander took over. He became known as Alexander the Great. As a Roman colony, Philippi was an important post on the Via Egnatia, a road that crossed Macedonia between what is now Turkey and the Adriatic Sea. Today, Philippi is an archaeological site near the city of Filippoi.

The Pineiós River flows down from the Pindus Mountains, cutting Thessaly in two. Before it reaches the Aegean Sea, the Pineiós courses through a deep, lush gorge called the Vale of Tempe. Here, it's said, the god Apollo fell in love with the nymph Daphne, who then changed into a laurel tree to escape him.

The region south of Thessaly is called Central Greece. It's the nation's most heavily populated region. Many mountains rise in Central Greece. One is Mount Parnassus, the site of ancient Delphi. The city of Thebes was once a powerful Greek city-state. On the region's southern end is the Attica Peninsula, the location of Athens, the nation's capital. Athens was a center of ancient Greek culture and is today the nation's largest city. It rests in a basin surrounded by mountains. Athens's Port of Piraeus is Greece's major port.

## The Peloponnese

Southern Greece consists of the Peloponnese peninsula, or simply the Peloponnese. It looks something like a leaf with four lobes connected to the mainland by a slender stem. Until a century ago, the Peloponnese was connected to the mainland by a narrow strip of land called the Isthmus of Corinth. But in the 1890s, a canal was cut through the isthmus. The Corinth Canal enabled large ships to travel between the Ionian Sea to the west and the Aegean Sea to the east.

In the center of the Peloponnese are the mountains and high plains of an area called Arcadia. Mountains extend out from Arcadia into each section of the peninsula. Pine forests and tough shrubs cover most of the Peloponnese, but crops grow on the fertile coastal plains.

The Peloponnese is the site of many of Greece's well-known ancient cities, such as Corinth, Mycenae, Epidaurus, Sparta, and Olympia. Their monuments and ruins offer fascinating insights into ancient life and religious beliefs. On the northern edge of the peninsula, the major cities are Corinth and Patras, Greece's third-largest city. On the east coast is Náfplio (previously Nauplia), Greece's first capital after gaining independence.

People have been living on the site of Patras for four thousand years. It is one of many ancient cities on the Peloponnese.

## Looking at Greece's Cities

Thessaloníki, also known as Salonika, is Greece's second-largest city, with a population of 322,240. More than one million people live in its metropolitan area. It is the major city of northern Greece and the capital of the Central Macedonia region. Along with Constantinople (today's Istanbul, Turkey), Thessaloníki was the co-capital of the Byzantine Empire (300s–1400s CE).

Thessaloníki is a major industrial center, with many chemical and steel plants, flour mills, textile mills, and shipyards. Cargo ships chug in and out of its bustling port on the Aegean Sea's Gulf of Thérmai. Culture and entertainment animate the city. People come from all over Greece to attend its theaters, operas, concerts, and international film festival. The Archaeological Museum of Thessaloníki houses ancient Macedonian artifacts, and the Museum of Byzantine Culture highlights centuries of Byzantine traditions.

Patras, the third-largest city in Greece with a population of 214,580 people, is perched on the northern edge of the Peloponnese. The city overlooks the Ionian Sea's Gulf of Patras and operates a busy port. Sunbathers enjoy its sandy beaches. Patras has been an important port city since ancient times. The ancient Romans established a colony there, and the Odeon, a Roman theater, still stands from that time. More recently, Patras was the scene of the first revolt in Greece's 1821 war for independence. Today, Patras is a major center for trade, communications, and technology. Its weeks-long Carnival in February is one of the most colorful in Europe, with spectacular costume balls, floats, and parades.

Iráklion (also known as Heraklion; above), the largest city on the island of Crete, is the nation's fourth-largest

city. Nearby are the ruins of the ancient city of Knossos. It was the center of the Minoan civilization that flourished for hundreds of years. Many Minoan artifacts now rest in the Heraklion Archaeological Museum. The city was named for the mythological hero Heracles, who saved Crete from a raging bull by seizing its horns. From this legend comes the saying "taking the bull by the horns," which means taking command or taking control.

The current city was founded almost 1,200 years ago by Arab Muslims who had been forced out of Spain. Since then, Iráklion has been under Byzantine, Venetian, Ottoman, and finally Greek control. Buildings from each of its historic eras remain in the city today.

Churches with bright blue domes stand out among the whitewashed buildings on the island of Santorini.

### The Islands

About 6,000 Greek islands are scattered throughout the Aegean and Ionian Seas. They range from little rocky nubs to large land-masses. People live on only about 227 of these islands, though. And only a few dozen islands have more than 100 residents.

Most of Greece's islands lie in the Aegean Sea, and most of these are rocky and arid. Neat, whitewashed houses, set high on the hillsides, sparkle in the sunlight. The inhabited islands have a harbor in a sheltered bay, with the main town built on a hillside. The Cyclades island group lies off Greece's southeast coast. The name comes from *kyklos*, the Greek word for "circle." The Cyclades forms a ring around Delos, a sacred place for ancient Greeks. Now its islands are popular holiday spots—especially Santorini, Mýkonos, Páros, and Náxos. Some people believe Santorini is the site of the legendary continent of Atlantis. Excavations have turned up a fabulous ancient city called Akrotíri, adding fuel to the legend.

The Dodecanese islands lie near the coast of Turkey. *Dodecanese* comes from the Greek word for "twelve," and there are a dozen major islands in the group. Rhodes, off the southwest tip of Turkey, is the largest. It's called the Island of Roses, though the bright red flowers that typically grow there are hibiscus.

The Aegean island of Crete is the largest of all the Greek islands and the fifth-largest island in the Mediterranean. It lies directly south of the Peloponnese, and its capital, Iráklion, is on the north coast. Crete's most famous site is Knossos, the center of Greece's prehistoric Minoan civilization.

Another island group is the Northern Sporades, which includes Sámos, Chios, Lésbos, and Límnos. They're located north of the Dodecanese. Across the Aegean, the large island of Euboea hugs the mainland coast. It's usually considered part of Central Greece. Off Euboea's coast is the Southern Sporades.

### The Colossus of Rhodes

In the early 200s BCE, Rhodes was the site of one of the Seven Wonders of the Ancient World. The Colossus of Rhodes was a gigantic statue whose legs, according to legend, straddled the harbor of the city of Rhodes. An earthquake destroyed the 98-foot (30 m) statue around 226 BCE. Now two bronze deer guard the harbor.

West of Greece's mainland are the islands of the Ionian Sea. The people who live on these islands enjoy a mild climate, with plenty of rainfall in the fall and winter. Farmers grow wheat, olives, grapes, and citrus fruits. With Italy just across the sea to the west, these islands have been influenced by Italian culture. Corfu is the largest and most populated Ionian island. Ithaca is remembered as the home of Ulysses in the Greek poet Homer's epic *The Odyssey*. Kíthira, far south of the other islands, lies off the southern tip of the Peloponnese.

## Climate

**A dip in the sea is refreshing during the hot Greek summers.**

Greece is sunny and bright, with brilliantly clear skies and cool sea breezes. Most of the country enjoys a Mediterranean

## Earthquakes and Volcanoes

Earthquakes have been Greece's worst natural disasters. Earthquakes are caused by the shifting movements of huge chunks of Earth's outer layer. These are called tectonic plates.

In the year 856 CE, a quake near Corinth destroyed the city and killed about 45,000 people. A 1953 quake in the Ionian Islands left 455 people dead and destroyed most of the houses. Athens suffered a severe earthquake in September 1999. It killed 143 people and left more than 100,000 homeless. Building codes are strictly enforced to keep earthquake damage to a minimum.

The same shifting plates have caused volcanic eruptions throughout Greece's history. Several ancient writers described the eruption of the Methana volcano near Athens in 230 BCE. The island of Santorini is actually the rim of an ancient volcano. An eruption around 1500 BCE blew the top off the volcano, leaving only the crater's edge. This ended the thriving Minoan civilization. Lava flows from this site were recorded as late as 1950.

climate. That means it's hot and dry in the summertime and mild and wet in the winter. Generally, it's much cooler in the mountains than along the coasts. July and August are the warmest months, while the coldest are December, January, and February. An icy wind called the boreas sweeps down from the north in the winter. It chills Thessaloníki, though it never reaches as far south as Crete. Winds from the south, called the sirocco, keep southern Greece warm.

Winds blowing in from the west bring most of Greece's rain and snow. Once the winds hit the central mountains, they cool off and change to moisture. That's why the western mountain slopes are more lush and green than the eastern side. Northwestern Greece is the wettest region, and the southeast is the driest. Rain, when it comes, is often a quick downpour that clears up just as fast. Snowfall in the mountains creates perfect ski conditions for winter holidays. Some of Greece's highest peaks keep their snowy caps almost year-round.

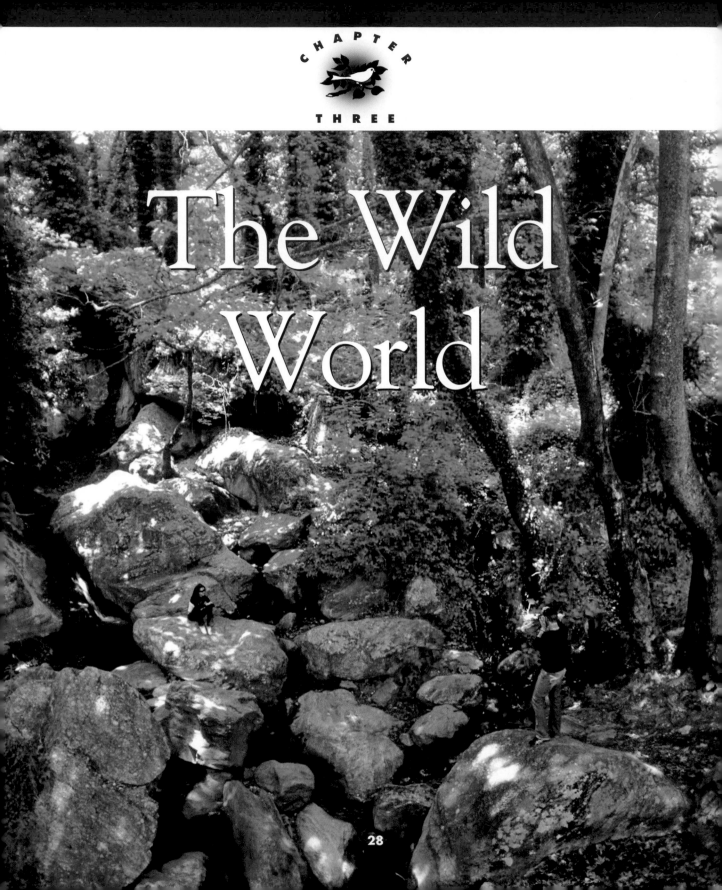

# The Wild World

S TROLL ALONG A ROAD IN THE GREEK COUNTRYSIDE, and you may notice a sharp, tangy smell in the air. That could mean that eucalyptus trees are nearby. Rows of eucalypti turn country roads into cool, shady lanes. Plane trees and pepper trees, which look like weeping willows, also provide roadside shade. Cypress trees are tall, thin evergreens that grow naturally along the coast. People also plant them in stately rows along roads or walkways.

*Opposite:* **Towering trees provide welcome shade in Greece.**

## Forests and Maquis

Mixed forests that include both evergreen of deciduous (leaf-shedding) trees grow near the coasts. Aleppo pines are a common sight on the rocky coastal slopes. Their trunks are twisted and their bark is gray. On the mountainsides are deciduous forests of maples, chestnuts, beeches, planes, and elms. Pines, Grecian firs, and other evergreens grow in the higher elevations.

Almost all of Greece was covered with forests in ancient times. Little by little, trees were cleared to make room for farming. Much of the wood was used for shipbuilding. Nibbling

### Athena's Gift

Greeks have been growing olive trees since ancient times. These trees, with their knobby trunks and silvery leaves, are considered the national tree. Olive trees grow almost everywhere in Greece except in the mountains. They don't grow very tall, but they live a long time. Today, some of the country's gnarled olive trees are a thousand years old!

According to Greek mythology, Athena and Poseidon argued over who should be the guardian of Athens. They agreed that whoever gave the city the best gift should win. Poseidon struck the earth, and the gift of water gushed forth. Athena kicked the ground, and up sprang an olive tree. The other gods declared Athena the winner, for her gift was more valuable.

goats took their toll on the foliage, too. Many regions that were once forested are now covered with only scrubby brush.

Today, forests cover about one-fifth of the country. Northern Greece is the most heavily wooded area. The Vasilítsa region in the northern Pindus Mountains is the largest and densest forestland in the country. It's rich with plant and animal life and is a favorite haunt for hikers and rock climbers.

A type of vegetation called maquis covers much of Greece, especially in the Peloponnese. Maquis consists of trees and shrubs with thick, shiny, leathery leaves. They tend to grow in a bushy shape and rarely grow more than 10 feet (3 m) high. When fire destroys a forest, maquis is often the first vegetation to take over. One example of it is gorse, a shrub with brilliant yellow flowers. Another is the mastic tree. If fire burns the mastic, its blackened trunk will recover and sprout again within a year. In time, holm oaks and pines sprout above this undergrowth. Holm oaks, or holly oaks, have shiny evergreen leaves and often grow in clumps.

In the drier southeast grow cactus, agave, and other succulents—plants that can store water to survive. People sometimes use succulents such as prickly pear cacti and aloe plants to mark the boundaries of their fields. Short, woody plants, many

**Prickly pear cactus produces small round fruits that are used to make juice, jellies, and other foods.**

of them with thorns, also survive well in dry, rocky soil. Their thorns help to hold moisture, and their deep roots find water far below the surface. Many wild herbs flourish when it's hot and dry, too. In the countryside, the summer air is sweet with the aroma of wild rosemary, sage, oregano, and thyme.

## Bountiful Blooms

Flowers played an important role in ancient Greek mythology, art, festivals, and daily life. Aphrodite—the goddess of love, beauty, and fertility—was said to bathe in sweet-smelling flowers. She made gardens grow, and any plant touched by her feet would burst into bloom. Ancient Greeks boiled flowers to make perfume, which both men and women wore.

Wildflowers carpet Greek meadows in the spring and again in the fall.

## The National Gardens

Visit Athens's National Gardens, and you'll stroll among free-roaming ducks, swans, and peacocks. This garden is in Athens's city center. It's a luxurious showcase for local species such as cypresses, Aleppo pines, olive trees, and orange trees. Broad avenues wind through the flower beds, leading past statues, ancient ruins, pavilions, pools, and even a small zoo.

The garden, originally named the Royal Gardens, was completed in 1840. Queen Amalia imported hundreds of exotic plant species for the park, but most of them died in the hot, dry climate. In 1974, the park was renamed the National Gardens and opened to the public. Today, it's home to more than five hundred species of trees, shrubs, and flowers.

In springtime, the meadows and hillsides of Greece are ablaze with wildflowers. Some are flowering herbs such as thyme, rosemary, lavender, and Jerusalem sage. There are violets, narcissi, oleanders, starlike anemones, wild orchids, tall spires of hibiscus, brilliantly colored rhododendrons, climbing bougainvilleas, and hardy rockroses. Irises, crocuses, and tulips grow high in the mountains in the cool shade of firs and pines, while scarlet poppies sprout up on the rockiest hillsides.

## Wild Animals

As Greece's forests have dwindled, so have the wild animals that made their homes there. Deer, brown bears, and wildcats still lurk in Greece's forests, especially in the north. On rare occasions, one might see wild boars, wolves, and lynxes. Foxes and badgers are more common. They creep through the forests and scrublands looking for prey such as mice and squirrels. Hares and porcupines, which live farther south, have adapted to hot, dry conditions.

Wild sheep and goats can sometimes be seen on the rocky hillsides. One very old species of goat lives on the island of

Both male and female bezoar goats have horns, though the males' horns are typically longer.

Crete. Called the wild bezoar goat (or bezoar ibex), it has a thick, woolly coat and long horns that curve backward. It is believed to have lived on the Greek islands since prehistoric times and to be an ancestor of the modern domestic goat.

## Creatures of the Sea and Air

Mother tortoises and loggerhead turtles bury their eggs on Greece's sandy beaches. But they don't stay to care for their young. The hot sun keeps the eggs warm, and the newly hatched turtles flop across the beach to make their own way into the sea. Growing cities and tourism have been threatening these seaside breeding grounds. On Zákynthos Island,

## Life as a Loggerhead

Loggerhead sea turtles are saltwater reptiles with large heads and powerful jaws. Their limbs are flippers, which enable them to swim swiftly and smoothly through the water. Adults usually weigh around 300 pounds (135 kilograms), but some have been known to reach 1,000 pounds (450 kg). Likewise, adults grow to be about 3 feet (1 m) long, but they can grow as long as 9 feet (3 m). They live fifty years or more.

At about thirty to thirty-five years of age, female loggerheads mate. Then they come ashore on a sandy beach and lay their eggs at night. Each female has about four nights of laying eggs, spaced two weeks apart, depositing more than one hundred eggs at a

time into a hole she digs with her flippers. Predatory animals and careless tourists destroy many of the eggs. The surviving hatchlings flop across the beach into the water. Three decades later, females return to the same beach where they hatched to lay their own eggs.

Loggerhead sea turtles are an endangered species. They have been captured for their meat, eggs, fat, and leathery skin. Those around Zákynthos Island are especially vulnerable to motorboats, fishnets, water pollution, and other human factors. The Zákynthos airport now bans nighttime flights to keep airplane noises from disturbing the nesting turtles.

**Many kinds of fish, including the sarpa salpa, swim in the waters off Greece.**

around Laganas Bay, is a loggerhead turtle breeding beach. It is now protected as a national marine park.

Many of Greece's sea creatures end up on the dinner table. They include octopus, squid, shellfish, and lobsters. Sardines, tuna, mackerel, bass, and mullet are some of Greece's common edible fish. Swimmers have to watch out for sharks and moray eels near the rocky coasts. They also avoid sea urchins and jellyfish, which can inflict painful stings.

Magpies, house sparrows, and blackbirds are common bird species in Greece. Nuthatches, blackcap warblers, and bee-eaters flit through the wooded hills, while partridges and quail scratch for insects on the forest floor. Soaring high overhead are eagles, falcons, vultures, and hawks. Along the coasts there are sea swallows, gulls, oyster fishers, pelicans, and herons.

Thousands of bird species pass through Greece on their migrations. Others come to settle in for the winter. Greece's wetlands make it a popular stopping place for birds. The Évros and Néstos Rivers of Thrace widen into marshy deltas as they reach the sea. As many as one hundred thousand birds migrate from northern Europe and Asia to spend their winters in these marshy regions. These and many other wetlands are protected areas.

### Playful Mammals

Images of dolphins appear on a lot of ancient Greek wall paintings, pottery, and coins. These beautiful sea mammals enjoy interacting with humans and often swim alongside boats. Out in the open waters, they can be seen leaping up in graceful arches.

Unofficially, the dolphin is considered Greece's national animal. Four kinds of dolphins live in Greek waters: bottlenose dolphins, striped dolphins (left), common dolphins, and Risso's dolphins. The largest are bottlenose dolphins. Because they often swim close to shore, they are the most familiar to humans. A large colony of bottlenose dolphins lives in the Amvrakikós Gulf on the western coast. Their numbers are decreasing, though. Pollution of the coast and waters is harming their habitat.

# Ancient Past, Modern Nation

H UMANS HAVE LIVED IN WHAT IS NOW GREECE for tens of thousands of years. Pockets of people in different regions developed their own unique civilizations, or ways of life. Among the earliest civilizations were the Minoans and the Mycenaeans.

The Minoans flourished on the island of Crete from about 2700 BCE to 1400 BCE. They are named after the legendary King Minos. According to mythology, Minos kept a labyrinth, or maze, in which there lurked a fearsome monster called the Minotaur, with a man's body and a bull's head. Every year, Minos sent victims into the labyrinth for the Minotaur to devour.

The Minoans were farmers, merchants, warriors, and sea-farers who carried on sea trade with other people around the Mediterranean. They used a form of writing called Linear A as well as hieroglyphics, or picture writing. Archaeologists have discovered a palace at Knossos, the Minoans' cultural center. Its many rooms and winding hallways may have been the basis for the tale of the Minotaur.

*Opposite:* **The Minoans were accomplished potters. This pot dates back more than four thousand years.**

A clay tablet with Linear B script. Linear B included about two hundred symbols. Some stood for syllables, while others stood for ideas.

Meanwhile, on the mainland, people were migrating into Greece from the north. Around 2000 BCE, the Achaeans, the first Greek people, began arriving. Other Greek groups such as the Ionians and the Aeolians followed. The civilization they developed is today called the Mycenaean civilization.

These early Greeks set up farming villages and introduced the gods that would become the basis of Greek religion. They left behind many documents written in a language that is now called Linear B. The language resembles the language now known as Greek.

Storytellers from this time passed down tales about the exploits of great kings and valiant heroes. Their stories tell of King Agamemnon, Achilles, and the Trojan War. Centuries later, Homer used such stories as the basis of his epic poems *The Iliad* and *The Odyssey*.

Mycenaean civilization fell around 1100 BCE, possibly as a result of an invasion by the Dorians, another group from the north. Greece then entered a dark age—a period that we know little about, which lasted three or four hundred years. Sometime between 1000 and 800 BCE, the Greeks began to disperse to the nearby lands around the Mediterranean Sea and establish Greek colonies. This dispersion is called the diaspora, a term still used for the scattering of people far from their homeland.

## The Rise of City-States

Around 800 to 750 BCE Greeks began banding together to form independent city-states. Each city-state had its own form of government. Among the strongest city-states were Athens and Sparta. Athens was making its fortune on the sea trade. Meanwhile, Sparta became a powerful warrior state. Like other city-states, the two often fought each other.

As masters of the sea, Greeks began establishing colonies around the Mediterranean region. Greek settlements grew up as far away as Italy, the island of Sicily, Spain, France, North Africa, Asia Minor (present-day Turkey), and Syria. Meanwhile, Greeks were holding athletic contests. In 776 BCE, the first Olympic games were held at Olympia. Around this

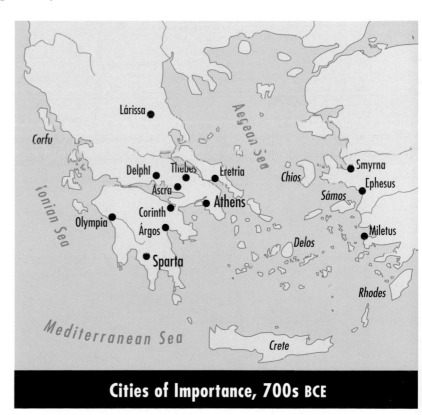

**Cities of Importance, 700s BCE**

same time, Homer was collecting centuries-old heroic tales and turning them into epic poems.

Although the city-states were developing sports, literature, and other refined pursuits, all was not peaceful. Typically, a tyrant wielded unlimited and brutal power over his city-state. Eventually, the citizens of the city-state would revolt and overthrow the tyrant. Then, for a while, a group of prominent citizens would rule. This joint rule by a few people is called an oligarchy.

Greeks fought Persians in the Battle of Salamis in the waters near Athens in 480 BCE.

## The First Marathon

According to legend, after the Greeks beat the Persians at the Battle of Marathon, a runner named Pheidippides was sent to Athens to report news of the victory. He ran the 26-mile (42-kilometer) distance nonstop and burst into the assembly. *"Nenikékamen!"* he shouted—"We have won!" Then he dropped dead from exhaustion. Modern marathon races are named in honor of Pheidippides's feat.

In 508 BCE, Athens broke this pattern. It threw its tyrant out and declared itself a democracy, a form of government in which power rests with the people. All free adult men would be able to vote on measures the city-state would adopt. This bold move would echo throughout history and inspire countless people to fight for democracy.

When the Persians, from western Asia, invaded Greece in 492 BCE, the city-states were forced to band together to fight their common enemy. In 490 BCE, the Greeks trounced the Persians in the Battle of Marathon. More attacks by the Persians brought on battles at Thermopylae and Salamis. One final Greek victory, at Plataea in 479 BCE, put an end to the threat posed by the Persians.

Unfortunately, the rivalry between the city-states of Athens and Sparta turned into the Peloponnesian War (431–404 BCE). Each of these city-states feared the other's growing power. After a series of bloody battles and a devastating siege, Athens surrendered to Sparta in 404 BCE.

## The Parthenon

The Parthenon is Classical Greece's greatest landmark. It stands atop the Acropolis, a complex of dozens of temples and sanctuaries dedicated to the goddess Athena, the guardian of Athens. An architect and sculptor named Phidias designed the complex, relying on a team of skilled artists and craftspeople. The Parthenon is the site's main temple honoring Athena.

Measuring about 228 x 101 feet (70 x 31 m), the Parthenon is surrounded on all sides by columns more than 34 feet (10 m) high. Inside, there was once a 40-foot (12 m) statue of Athena sculpted out of gold and ivory. The gold was removed after about 150 years to pay for military expenses. The statue continued to stand until the fifth century CE. The most stunning part of the temple was the frieze—a long scene carved in marble around the outside of the building.

The Parthenon remained intact until 1687, when it was severely damaged in a war. In the early 1800s, the British earl of Elgin removed much of the Parthenon's remains and took them to the British Museum in London. That included most of the remaining frieze, as well as a caryatid, or female statue that served as a column, from the nearby Erechtheum temple. Greece demands the return of these artifacts, known as the Elgin Marbles or the Parthenon Marbles. But the British Museum so far has refused.

## The Golden Age

Despite its wars, Greece was developing a high level of civilization. The fifth century BCE (400s BCE) marked the peak of Greece's Classical period, or golden age. This was a time when art, architecture, literature, philosophy, and science flourished. Athens became the major political power and cultural center of the Greek world.

The glories of the golden age are mainly the work of a statesman named Pericles. He ruled Athens for more than thirty years—from 461 to 429 BCE. One of Pericles's greatest achievements was rebuilding the Acropolis. This sacred site on a hilltop in Athens had been destroyed during the Persian Wars. Pericles had dozens of temples and sanctuaries built. The most fabulous was the Parthenon, the main temple of Athena. The temples were adorned with sculptures. Some of these artifacts remain in place today, while others have been removed to museums throughout the world.

Pericles loved the arts and sciences and encouraged creativity. Classical Greek thinkers include the philosophers Socrates, Plato, and Aristotle. They laid the foundations for logical thinking. Playwrights flourished, too. Aeschylus, Sophocles, and Euripides wrote tragedies, and Aristophanes wrote comedies. Their works are still performed today. Every drama or comedy on TV or in the theater today follows the dramatic principles they established. The historian Herodotus described much of what we know about the conflicts between the Greeks and the Persians. Other greats were the historian Thucydides, the physician Hippocrates, the

## Ancient Greeks Who Paved the Way

Archimedes (ca. 287–212 BCE) was a scientist whose inventions included war machines and a screw for raising water out of a river. He's famous for springing out of a bathtub and shouting *"Eureka!"* ("I have found it!"). While in the tub, he had figured out how to calculate the weight of an object floating in water.

Hippocrates (ca. 460–ca. 377 BCE) was the first doctor to use scientific methods to find the causes of illnesses. All doctors today take the Hippocratic oath, named after him. They swear to practice medicine honorably and to do no harm.

Socrates (ca. 470–399 BCE, right), a philosopher, taught his students critical thinking by breaking problems down into a series of questions. This method is now known as the Socratic method. His most famous student was Plato (ca. 428–ca. 348 BCE). Plato taught

idealism—the view that at the root of everything is an ideal concept.

Aristotle (384–322 BCE, left) was a student of Plato. He tried to gather all knowledge into one universal system. His method of arriving at sensible conclusions is called Aristotelian logic.

Pythagoras (ca. 570–ca. 500 BCE) devised a way to calculate the hypotenuse (the longest side, which is opposite the right angle) of a right triangle—$a^2 + b^2 = c^2$. It's still called the Pythagorean theorem. But it was Euclid (flourished ca. 300 BCE) who developed much of what is studied in geometry today, earning him the title the Father of Geometry.

geometry experts Pythagoras and Euclid, and the engineer and inventor Archimedes. They established the foundations for today's sciences.

## Alexander and the Hellenistic Period

The Peloponnesian War had weakened Greece, making it vulnerable to a takeover. Philip II, from the kingdom of Macedonia to the north, took advantage of the situation. By 338 BCE, he had fought his way through Greece and taken control of the region. After Philip's death, his young son Alexander gathered a well-trained Greek and Macedonian army. They went on to conquer the vast Persian Achaemenian Empire and much more. In only ten years, Alexander's empire stretched from the borders of China in the east to Egypt in the west. It is no wonder that Alexander became known as Alexander the Great.

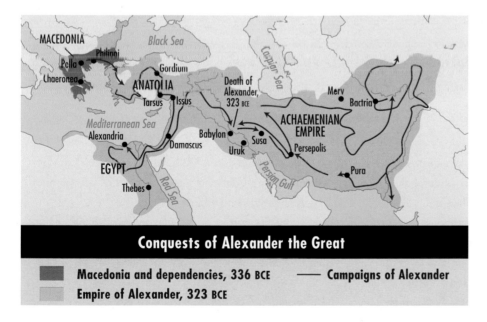

**Conquests of Alexander the Great**

Macedonia and dependencies, 336 BCE ⎯⎯ Campaigns of Alexander

Empire of Alexander, 323 BCE

## Alexander the Great

Alexander (356–323 BCE) studied under the Greek philosopher Aristotle until he was sixteen years old. He loved his trusty black stallion, Bucephalus, who carried him into all the great battles of his life.

After his father, Philip II of Macedonia, was assassinated in 336 BCE, Alexander became king and took command of the Macedonian and Greek army. With 35,000 troops, he conquered Persia, defeating the Persian king Darius at the Battle of Issus in 333 BCE. Then he conquered Egypt and founded the city of Alexandria in 332 BCE. Next he took Babylon (in today's Iraq) and then the areas of present-day Afghanistan and India.

By the age of thirty, Alexander ruled all of the world known to Greeks at the time. According to legend, Alexander then wept, for there were no worlds left for him to conquer. He died, of a fever or of poisoning, just before his thirty-third birthday.

After Alexander died in 323 BCE, his generals divided his empire among themselves. This is called the Hellenistic period. During this time, Greek art and culture spread throughout the empire.

*Winged Victory of Samothrace* is one of greatest pieces of Hellenistic sculpture. It is celebrated for its power and sense of movement.

### Under Roman Rule

Meanwhile, to the west, the Roman Empire was engaged in conquests of its own. Greece, so close to Roman lands, was a natural target. Romans gradually took control of Greek lands until they destroyed the ancient city of Corinth in 146 BCE. This was the final blow in the Roman conquest of Greece. Now Greece became just another province of the Roman Empire.

Under the Roman Empire, Greeks were free to pursue their usual arts and trades, as long as Rome reaped most of the profits. The Romans admired Greek culture, though. They adopted Greece's religion, arts, and customs as their own. Soon, the entire Roman Empire had taken on Greek ways. Greek gods and goddesses were given Roman names, but their roles stayed the same. In time, the new religion of Christianity would replace the Greek and Roman gods.

Neither Christianity nor Judaism was welcome in the Roman Empire because both religions challenged the authority of the emperors. In the first two centuries CE, Christians were executed by the thousands. That ended, however, when the emperor Constantine embraced Christianity.

## The Byzantine Period

In 330 CE, Constantine moved his capital from Rome to Byzantium, an ancient Greek colony in what is now Turkey. This marks the beginning of the Byzantine period. Soon, the city was renamed Constantinople. Constantine allowed freedom of religion. Later, Theodosius became emperor. In 393 or 394 CE, he made Christianity the official religion of the Roman Empire and put an end to the Olympic games.

The vast Roman Empire split into eastern and western halves in 395. Under attack by Germanic tribes, the Western Roman Empire fell in 476. The Eastern Roman Empire carried on as the Byzantine Empire, with Constantinople as its capital and Greek as its official language. Christianity, too, developed in two halves, with Western Christianity using Rome's Latin language and Eastern Christianity using Greek.

Despite the battles and upheaval, Greeks carried on with daily life. Thessaloníki, Thebes, and Corinth became thriving industrial centers. Monasteries were built throughout the empire, many adorned with lavish artwork.

Relations between Eastern and Western Christianity were often tense. The patriarch of Constantinople led the Eastern Church, while the pope in Rome headed the Western Church.

Byzantine churches feature colorful artwork, often decorated with gold.

In 1054, the two broke apart permanently. They continued as the Roman Catholic Church in the West and the Greek Orthodox Church in the East.

### Ottoman Rule

Meanwhile, the religion of Islam was spreading outward from its birthplace on the Arabian Peninsula. Armies of Muslims spread their faith. Muslim Turkish armies united as the Ottoman Empire and gradually took over more and more Byzantine lands. By the late 1300s, the Ottomans occupied much of the Balkan Peninsula, including large parts of

Greece. In 1453, the Ottomans seized Constantinople. After more than 1,100 years of power, the Byzantine Empire collapsed. In Greece itself, Athens fell in 1458. The Peloponnese held out against the Ottomans until 1460.

The Ottomans allowed the Greek Orthodox Church to carry on. This helped Greeks keep their sense of national identity alive. Greek was the language of the church, and religious festivals were an important part of Greek culture.

The Ottomans trained promising young Greek men for their army and for government jobs. The economy prospered as Greek merchants carried trade from Spain in the west all the way to

The Ottoman siege of Constantinople, from April to May of 1453, brought about the end of the Byzantine Empire.

ports on the Black Sea in the east. But at the same time, taxes became more and more burdensome for ordinary peasants, and they began staging revolts. Peasant bandits called *klephts* lurked in the mountain passes to attack and rob Ottoman officials. Many popular songs glorified their bravery and heroic resistance.

## The War of Independence

By the late 1700s, Greek merchants made up a well-to-do middle class. To improve Greek schools, they sent teachers to study in western European universities. The Greek visitors were surprised to find that Europeans looked on ancient Greek culture with reverence and awe. Classical Greek and Roman art, sculpture, architecture, and literature had become models for western Europe's Renaissance, or "rebirth." When the Greek visitors returned home, they spread their newfound pride in Greek heritage.

Patriotic Greeks began forming secret societies to work for independence. One such society was led by General Alexander Ypsilantis. With his encouragement, Greeks staged a major revolt. Fierce Greek fighters stormed down from the northern mountains into the Peloponnese in 1821. They battered one Ottoman stronghold after another, setting up local governments as they went along. This began the War of Greek Independence. Eventually, Great Britain, France, and Russia banded together on Greece's side. The war ended with the Battle of Navarino in 1827, in which Greece and its allies defeated the Ottoman navy. By 1828, the powerful nations of the world accepted Greece as a new, independent nation.

The people of Nauplia greet King Otto as he enters the capital city.

At the time of independence, Greece was less than half the size it is today. Much of its ancient territory remained in the hands of the Ottomans and other powers. Nevertheless, Greeks established a capital at Nauplia (now called Náfplio) and got on with the business of government. They elected Ioánnis Kapodístrias as their first prime minister, but he was assassinated within a couple of years. Great Britain, France, and Russia—together called the Great Powers—had pledged to oversee the new country until it got on its feet. In 1833, they installed a seventeen-year-old prince named Otto as king. Otto wielded absolute power and ruled unwisely. So in 1844, Greeks forced him to make the country a constitutional monarchy, with a national assembly and a prime minister. He continued to rule with unlimited power, however, until Greeks forced him from the throne in 1862.

George I, a prince from the royal family of Denmark, came to the throne in 1864. Under his more democratic reign, Greece wrote a new constitution and increased trade. The country's progress was stalled, however, by a disastrous war with the Ottoman Empire. Greece entered the twentieth century much weakened. Despite this, in the next few years, Greece was able to double its size.

## Troubled Times

The Ottoman Empire fell apart at the end of World War I (1914–1918). The victors asked Greece to provide an army to keep the peace between the Turks and minorities in western Turkey. This resulted in another bloody war between Greece and Turkey, the heir of the Ottoman Empire. The Greek army was defeated, and more than 1,300,000 Greeks were forced from Turkey. The Greek refugees, leaving lands where their families had lived for two thousand years, settled in Greece.

The influx of refugees and a severe economic downturn in the 1930s created great political instability. In 1936, General Ioannis Metaxas took over and established a dictatorship.

**Development of Modern Greece, 1832–1947**

| | |
|---|---|
| Kingdom of Greece, 1832 | Acquisitions, 1913 |
| Acquisitions, 1863 | Acquisitions, 1919 |
| Acquisitions, 1881 | Acquisitions after 1920 |

Germany brutally occupied Greece during World War II (1939–1945). Following the war, a bloody civil war broke out (1946–1949), with Greek communists fighting government forces. The government forces eventually won.

In 1967, military officers again seized power. The seven years of military dictatorship that followed wrecked the economy and brought Greece and Turkey to the brink of war. In 1974, the military invited former prime minister Konstantinos Karamanlis back to rule the country. Democratic rule was restored the following year.

This marked the beginning of a new era of political stability for Greece. Two major political parties emerged—the Panhellenic Socialist Movement (PASOK) and the New Democracy (ND) party. Since then, leadership has passed back and forth between the two parties. Greece joined the European Economic Community, now called the European Union (EU), in 1981.

## The Debt Crisis

At the beginning of the twenty-first century, Greece had one of the strongest, most stable economies in Europe. Like many other countries, though, Greece was caught up in the worldwide financial crisis of the early 2000s.

In 2000, Greece joined the Eurozone. That is the group of EU countries using the euro as currency. All Eurozone members agreed to follow certain guidelines to keep the zone financially strong and healthy. All, including Greece, agreed to keep their national debts low. They also agreed to a low annual budget deficit—that is, government spending would not be much higher than government income.

Greece kept borrowing and spending, however. The government hid its financial situation by reporting false economic figures for several years. But by 2010, the truth was out: Greece's debts and deficits were among the highest in the world. Now Greece's financial crisis threatened to damage other banks in the Eurozone and destroy the value of the euro.

To help bring down the deficit, the government proposed higher taxes and drastic spending cuts, including lower salaries and retirement benefits for government employees. Violent protests against these measures erupted in Athens and other cities in May 2010. More riots swept the country in 2011.

Many Greeks took to the streets in 2011 to protest budget cuts and other steps the government planned to take to deal with the nation's economic crisis.

Eurozone leaders tried out many ideas for stabilizing Greece's finances. But as of spring 2012, the economy was still in trouble, and there were discussions that Greece might leave the Eurozone. Regardless of its financial troubles, one thing is certain—in the birthplace of democracy, democracy is here to stay.

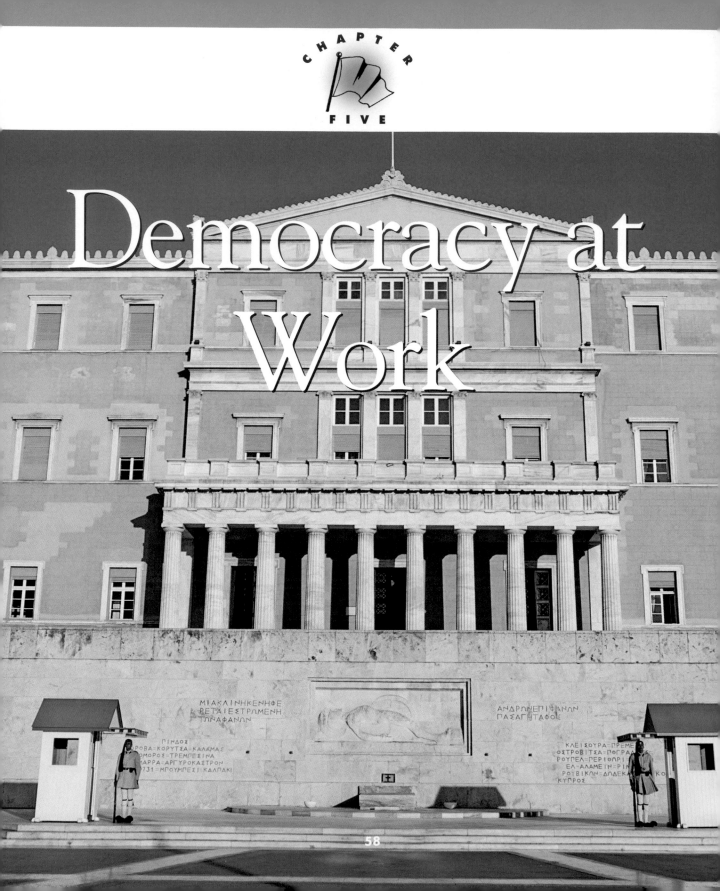

# Democracy at Work

G REECE IS KNOWN AS THE BIRTHPLACE OF DEMOCRACY. In a democracy, the citizens participate in the decisions that affect their lives. Greece's democratic ideals inspired the founders of the United States. And millions of people around the world have fought and died to obtain a democratic form of government.

Ancient Athens had what is called a direct democracy. Individual citizens gathered in Athens to vote directly on proposed laws. Today, so many people live in most nations that direct democracy does not work well. Instead, many countries have representative democracies, where the citizens elect representatives to carry out their wishes. This is also called a republic.

After Greece abolished its monarchy in 1975, it adopted its current constitution. The constitution declared Greece's form of

*Opposite:* **The Greek Parliament meets in a stately building on Syntagma Square.**

## The National Anthem

"Ýmnos eis tin Eleftherian" ("Ode to Liberty") is Greece's national anthem. Adopted as the national anthem in 1865, it is the first two stanzas of a 158-verse poem written in 1823 by Dionysios Solomos, a poet from Zákynthos Island. Nikolaos Mantzaros composed the music. This anthem is played during the closing ceremonies of all Olympic Games to honor Greece as the birthplace of the Olympics.

| **Greek lyrics** | **English translation** |
|---|---|
| Se gnorízo apó tin kópsi | I recognize you by the fearful |
| tou spathiou tin tromer, | edge of your sword, |
| se gnorízo apó tin ópsi, | I recognize you from your countenance |
| pou me via metrái tin gi. | that measures the earth. |
| | |
| Ap' ta kókkala vgalméni | You sprang from sacred |
| ton Ellínon ta ierá, | Greek bones, valiant as |
| kai san próta andrioméni, | in the past, greetings |
| hére, o hére, elefthériá! | Liberty, hail! |

government a parliamentary republic. It also provided for three branches of government: legislative, executive, and judicial.

### Legislative Branch

Greece's lawmaking body is a 300-member parliament. The parliament is unicameral, meaning it has only one house. This differs from the two-house legislatures of the United States, Canada, the United Kingdom, and many other nations. Greece's members of parliament are elected to four-year terms. By law, all citizens over age eighteen must vote, but this is not enforced. The people elect 288 members of parliament by direct vote. The other 12 members are chosen according to how many votes each political party receives.

## The National Flag

The national flag of Greece features nine horizontal stripes, alternating blue and white. In the upper left corner is a white cross upon a field of blue. Many people believe the nine stripes stand for the nine syllables in the phrase *"Elefthériá i Thanatos,"* meaning "Freedom or Death." The white cross stands for the Greek Orthodox Church, Greece's major religion. This flag was adopted in 1822.

## National Government of Greece

### Executive Branch

PRESIDENT

PRIME MINISTER

CABINET

### Legislative Branch

PARLIAMENT (300 MEMBERS)

### Judicial Branch

SPECIAL SUPREME TRIBUNAL

SUPREME COURT OF CIVIL AND PENAL LAW

COUNCIL OF STATE

COURTS OF APPEAL

COURTS OF FIRST INSTANCE

The president is Greece's head of state. He or she is elected every five years. Instead of being elected by the people, a Greek president is elected by members of parliament. The constitution limits the president's powers. Most executive power belongs to the prime minister.

After an election, the president appoints the prime minister, who is officially the head of government. The prime minister must be the leader of the political party that has the most seats in the parliament. So, in effect, voters are choosing the prime minister when they vote for members of parliament. If the parliament no longer agrees with the prime minister's

Karolos Papoulias became president of Greece in 2005 and was reelected in 2010.

### George Papandreou

Politics runs in George Papandreou's family. His grandfather, Georgios, was prime minister of Greece three times, and his father, Andreas, was prime minister twice and founded the Panhellenic Socialist Movement (PASOK) party.

George Papandreou was born in 1963 in St. Paul, Minnesota, where his father was teaching at a university. He moved to Greece in 1974 and was elected to parliament in 1981. He later held several cabinet posts, making advances in education, human rights, and foreign relations. In 2009, Papandreou became prime minister of Greece as leader of the PASOK party. During the debt crisis of 2010 to 2011, his economic policies were heavily criticized and he was forced to step down.

policies, its members may cast a vote of "no confidence." This took place during the 2011 debt crisis, when Prime Minister George Papandreou was voted out of office. In such a case, parliament chooses a new prime minister.

The prime minister leads the cabinet of ministers. The ministers oversee areas such as foreign affairs, the environment, defense, agriculture, labor, and culture and tourism. The prime minister recommends people for cabinet posts, and the president officially appoints them.

### Judicial Branch

Greece's courts are organized into three levels. The courts of first instance are the lower courts, where cases go first. If a person thinks the court made a mistake in a case, he or she can

A prisoner is brought into court. In most criminal cases, a panel made up of three professional judges and four jurors decides the outcome of a trial.

ask a court of appeal to review the decision. People can also appeal their cases to one of Greece's supreme courts, whose decisions are final.

Greece has three supreme courts. The Council of State is the highest court for administrative law. That includes matters such as government regulations, social security claims, and the legality of administrative laws. The Council of State has a president, ten vice presidents, and many judges.

The Supreme Court of Civil and Penal Law is the highest court for civil and criminal cases. It consists of a president, the attorney general, ten vice presidents, and dozens of judges who perform various duties.

The highest of the three supreme courts is the Special Supreme Tribunal. Its members are the presidents of the other two supreme courts plus several judges and legal experts. This court decides whether a law fits with Greece's constitution. It also resolves disputes over parliamentary elections, disputes between courts and government agencies, and conflicts between different courts' decisions.

## Political Parties

Greece has two major political parties: the Panhellenic Socialist Movement (PASOK) and the New Democracy (ND) party. They have been the leading parties since Greece reestablished democracy in 1975. The Panhellenic Socialist Movement favors taking care of people in need, international cooperation, and greater self-government at the local level. The New Democracy party supports social reforms and conservative economic policies.

Several other parties have elected members to parliament. They include the Communist Party of Greece, the Popular Orthodox Rally, and the Ecologist Greens.

## Regional and Local Government

As of January 1, 2011, Greece was reorganized to make local government simpler and more efficient. The new plan divides the country into seven large areas called decentralized administrations. Within each of these areas are one, two, or three

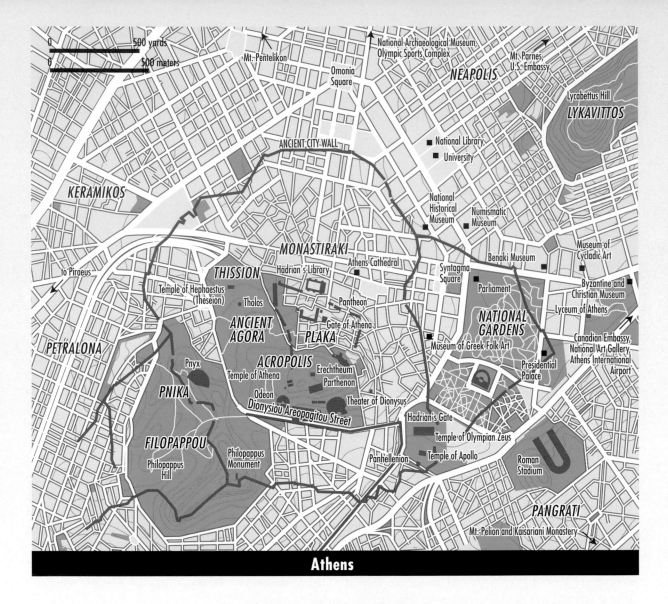

**Athens**

## Athens: The Capital City

Athens is Greece's capital and largest city. With a city population of 655,780 in 2011, it spreads outward into an urban area of more than 3,000,000 people. One of the oldest cities in the world, Athens has been inhabited nonstop for at least seven thousand years. The Mycenaeans first established a permanent settlement there around 1400 BCE. For many ancient civilizations

after that time, Athens was a center for trade, culture, and military power. Athens is also known as the birthplace of democracy, because the democratic form of government was first introduced there in 508 BCE.

Visitors can see many of Athens's greatest archaeological landmarks by traveling along Dionysiou Aeropagitou Street. They pass by the Temple of Olympian Zeus, the

the largest district, is home to the Parliament building, upscale department stores, and fine hotels. Visitors gather near the Parliament building to see the hourly changing of the costumed presidential guards (left).

Athens's largest museum is the National Archaeological Museum, with artifacts from thousands of years of Greek history. The Benaki Museum focuses on historic Greek culture, with branches devoted to Islamic art, children's toys, Chinese art, and other specialties. The Byzantine and Christian Museum houses Byzantine-era art, and the Numismatic Museum features historic coins.

Residents and visitors alike enjoy Athens's mild climate. Summers are warm and dry, and winters are cool and rainy. July is the hottest month, with an average high temperature of 92 degrees Fahrenheit (33 degrees Celsius). Very little rain falls in July and August. January, the coolest month, has an average low temperature of 44°F (7°C). The heaviest rains fall in December, January, and February.

Acropolis and Parthenon, the Temple of Hephaestus, and the Agora. Syntagma Square (Constitution Square),

peripheries, or regions, for a total of thirteen regions. Each region is governed by a governor and a council, with elections held every five years.

At the local level are 325 municipalities. Each municipality elects a mayor and a municipal council for five-year terms.

Mount Athos is one place that stands alone. It is not part of any region or decentralized administration. The monks in the monasteries of Mount Athos govern themselves, apart from any political interference.

# Fruits of Their Labor

A FARMER SPREADS OUT A LARGE NET AT THE BASE of an olive tree. Then he climbs a ladder and begins shaking the branches. Using a pole or a rake, he reaches up to scrape the upper branches. Olives rain down, and his children and neighbors scurry to whisk any stray olives into the center of the net. Once the tree is harvested, everyone helps in gathering up the net full of olives and heaving it into a basket. Then they move on to the next tree in the grove. If the olives are destined to become olive oil, they go to an olive mill within hours. There, a wheel-like stone crushes them and a press squeezes them to produce the thick, savory oil.

Greece's olive harvest begins in the fall. Some farmers use machines to harvest their crop. But in many places, the land is too hilly to bring in harvesting machines. Here the olives are harvested by hand, which keeps them from getting bruised.

## Agriculture

In terms of weight, Greece's largest crop is corn, followed by olives, wheat, and tomatoes. However, olives bring in the

A shepherd drives his flock along a road in Kefallinía. Sheep are raised for both milk and wool.

most farm income. Only Spain and Italy produce more olives than Greece, and Greek olives and olive oil are prized worldwide for their delicious taste.

Greece is also known for its zesty feta cheese, which is made from goat milk. In fact, Greek farmers produce millions of tons of sheep and goat milk, as well as fruits and nuts. In 2009, Greece ranked among the world's top ten producers of sheep milk, olives, kiwi fruit, peaches and nectarines, goat milk, pistachios, chestnuts, cotton, and almonds. Figs, sugar beets, watermelons, rice, and tobacco are important crops in Greece, too.

Farming accounts for only a little over 3 percent of Greece's total economic output. But farming requires a lot of time and human labor. About one-eighth of the Greek labor force works in agriculture. Harvesting olives is just one example of the complex farming activities that must be done by hand.

Greek farmers are hampered by rocky, mountainous terrain, poor soil, and low rainfall. Less than one-third of Greek land can be farmed. Large-scale farming takes place only in the regions of Thessaly, Macedonia, and Thrace. Greece's

overall farm production is steadily improving, though. As a member of the EU, Greece gets help through the EU's Common Agricultural Policy. This program has enabled Greece to improve its farming methods, productivity, crop prices, and quantity of exports.

### Manufacturing

Greece has a long tradition of manufacturing food products, textiles, and cement. Many of Greece's farm products are processed into foods such as wine made from grapes, olive oil made from olives, and dairy products such as cheese made from milk. Fruits and nuts are also dried and preserved for sale. Among Greece's textile products are cotton yarn and cloth, clothing, and carpeting. Greece also has a long-standing shoe industry.

A huge cement factory stands in Vólos. It produced much of the concrete block used in building the country's many concrete apartment buildings. Today, this facility is one of the largest cement factories in the world. Oil refining is another thriving industry in Greece. The refineries turn out jet fuels, motor oils, and liquefied petroleum gas.

**Many homes in Greece are made of concrete.**

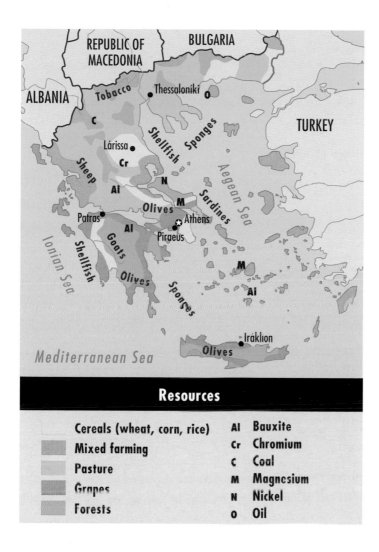

## Resources

| Cereals (wheat, corn, rice) | Al | Bauxite |
| Mixed farming | Cr | Chromium |
| Pasture | c | Coal |
| Grapes | M | Magnesium |
| Forests | N | Nickel |
| | o | Oil |

In this country with a long shipping tradition, Greek shipyards build huge cargo ships. Other factory goods include plastics, electronics, electrical machinery such as refrigerators, chemicals such as drugs, and aluminum metal processed from bauxite ore.

Greece faces stiff competition from countries that have their factory goods made in China. Thus, many Greek manufacturers are focusing on research to make their products more innovative and attractive.

## What Greece Grows, Makes, and Mines

**Agriculture (2009)**

| | |
|---|---|
| Corn | 2,353,000 metric tons |
| Olives | 1,963,190 metric tons |
| Wheat | 1,830,000 metric tons |

**Manufacturing (2008)**

| | |
|---|---|
| Petroleum products | 156,000,000 barrels |
| Cement | 15,000,000 metric tons |
| Foods and beverages | 756,000 metric tons |

**Mining (2009)**

| | |
|---|---|
| Lignite (coal) | 61,800,000 metric tons |
| Bauxite | 1,935,000 metric tons |
| Nickeliferous ores | 1,400,000 metric tons |

## Mining

Throughout the world are statues, columns, and palace and temple floors and walls made of Greek marble. This super-hard stone can be polished to a gleaming shine. Greek miners have been cutting marble from mountainsides and pits for thousands of years. The marble mining sites, called quarries, yield a dazzling variety of colors—red, green, black, white, pink, beige, and many more.

Marble may be Greece's most beautiful mining product, but its most valuable minerals have industrial uses. For example, most of

Greece's electrical energy comes from coal-burning power plants. Most of those plants use lignite, a soft, brown type of coal. That lignite comes from Greece's large natural deposits. Germany is the only EU country that produces more lignite than Greece. The nation's largest lignite deposits are located at Ptolemaïs and Amyntaio, in the northern part of the country. Lignite is also mined in the Megalopolis area in the Peloponnese.

Bauxite is the raw material used in producing aluminum. Most of Greece's bauxite is mined in Central Greece, among the Parnassus, Helicon, and Gióna mountains. On the world's markets, Greece is a leading supplier of bentonite, magnesite, and perlite. Greece also mines copper, lead, zinc, gold, silver, and nickeliferous ores, or materials that contain the metal nickel.

Marble is cut from the earth in large blocks so it can be used to make everything from countertops to statues.

## Economic Activities as Share of GDP* (2009)

| | |
|---|---|
| Services | 78.9% |
| Manufacturing | 10.3% |
| Construction | 4.6% |
| Agriculture | 3.2% |
| Mining | 0.4% |
| Other | 2.6% |

*The gross domestic product (GDP) is the total value of all goods and services a country produces in a year.

The Acropolis in Athens is the most visited archaeological site in Greece. The ruins of many ancient buildings stand on this flat-topped rock that overlooks the city.

## Tourism and Shipping

More than nineteen million tourists pour into Greece every year. They explore sites such as the Acropolis, with its temples and shrines; Rhodes, with its castles and mosques; and other ancient places, including Olympia, Mycenae, and Delphi. Tour guides, ferryboat captains, hotel employees, bus drivers, cooks, waiters, and many other people serve the needs of these tourists. They are all part of Greece's tourism industry, the largest sector of the nation's services industry. About 15 percent of Greece's income is from tourism. Tourists travel to Greece from countries all over the world, but most visitors come from Germany, the United Kingdom, and Italy.

Surrounded by water on three sides, Greece has always been a nation of seafarers. Today, shipping is still an important part of Greece's economy.

Greece's fleet of merchant ships is the largest in the world. Most of Greece's ships carry dry bulk cargo—that is, dry goods such as grains, ore, and cement. Others are tankers, which carry liquids such as oil, chemicals, and liquid natural gas. Many other Greek ships are container vessels. They carry huge metal containers that are transported later by truck or railroad.

Huge containers sit at the Port of Piraeus outside Athens. They will be loaded onto ships and carried all around the world.

## Austerity Measures

Because of its 2010 debt crisis, Greece began a policy of financial austerity, or strictness. That involved raising taxes and

In 2011, professors formed a chain blocking the University of Athens as a protest against cuts in the education budget.

cutting back on salaries and pensions for government employees. Many institutions in Greece are run by the government, including schools, hospitals, banks, post offices, electricity services, and TV and radio stations.

These measures affected a large number of low- and middle-class families. Employees saw their salaries decrease, their vacation and health care benefits disappear, and their old-age incomes drop. Many workers were cut from full-time to part-time schedules, and many others were laid off to save companies money. By January 2012, Greece's unemployment rate had risen to 21.8 percent. Things were even worse for young people under twenty-five years old. Their unemployment rate was 50.8 percent.

Government austerity meant that citizens had to make cutbacks at home. They cut their own spending on entertainment, clothing, and travel. With high gas prices, more people began taking public transportation. Many people lost their homes, too, because they could not keep up with their mortgage payments. Some families decided to move to another country where they might have a better chance of finding work. Economists predicted that it would be many years before Greece's economy returned to normal.

## Communications

Walk down a street in Greece, and you'll see a surprising number of people chatting on their cell phones. Mobile phone use in Greece is extremely high. In 2009, there were more than twenty million cell phones in use in Greece. That's almost twice the nation's entire population! Average cell phone users had more than two phones apiece. Use has dropped since then. Hoping to cut down on anonymous mobile phone calls, the government passed a law in 2009 requiring all mobile phone users to register their names and other identifying information. Still, Greece's cell phone usage compared to population remains among the highest in the world. In contrast, there are far fewer landline phones than cell phones in Greece.

About five million Greeks use the Internet. Those without their own Internet access use their school computers or take advantage of one of Greece's many Internet cafés.

In print media, the leading daily newspapers are *To Vima* (the Tribune), *Ethnos* (Nation), *Ta Nea* (the News), and *Kathimerini*

(Daily). The top weekly papers are *Proto Thema* (Lead Story), *Kathimerini tis Kyriakis* (Sunday Daily), and *Real News*. Most Greeks, however, look to television for their news and entertainment. The government controlled TV and radio broadcasting until 1989. Now people enjoy dozens of private stations, both broadcast and satellite. As in the United States and Canada, popular Greek TV shows range from news and sports to soap operas, reality shows, and movies.

## Transportation

Ride the Athens Metro, and you'll feel like you are exploring a museum. Many stations on this underground rapid transit system have marble floors and museum-style exhibits. There are sculptures, statues, modern art exhibits, archaeological treasures, and replicas of precious objects from antiquity. The Syntagma Square station shows a cutaway view of an archaeological dig that took place right on the spot. The Metro reaches all sectors of the city, and one line runs to the Athens International Airport.

Getting to Greece is easy. Athens and nine other Greek cities have international airports. Olympic Air and Aegean Airlines are the national airlines. Besides flying outside the country, these airlines also fly between many cities and towns within Greece. Getting around by road is easy, too. The Egnatia Highway runs across northern Greece from the Adriatic coast in the northwest to the Turkish border in the east. Roads connect major cities and towns and reach even remote villages.

The Corinth Canal runs between the mainland and the Peloponnese, and huge ferryboats make the crossing several times a day. The canal also gives easy access to the Port of Piraeus, the major port for Athens and the entire country. Patras and Thessaloníki are important ports, too.

A ship travels through the Corinth Canal, which was completed in 1893. The canal is only 70 feet (21 m) wide, too narrow for many modern ships to pass through it.

# People, Language, and Learning

I N 2011, ABOUT 10.8 MILLION PEOPLE LIVED IN GREECE. Most people in Greece live along the coasts and in the central plains. About 35 percent of Greece's entire population occupies the Attica region, which surrounds Athens, the largest city.

## Ethnic Groups and Immigrants

The great majority of the people in Greece are ethnic Greeks. Greece has always had many residents from other cultures, too. One long-standing ethnic group is a Muslim minority in Thrace. Since the late twentieth century, the country has had a heavy influx of immigrants. The newcomers seek safety and a better way of life.

Many of these newer immigrants are eastern Europeans from places such as Bulgaria, Romania, and Ukraine. Turmoil in the Balkans region drove in even more people. For example, conflicts in the former Yugoslavia in the 1990s forced Serbs and other ethnic groups to flee to nearby Greece. After

| Population of Major Cities (2011 est.) | |
| --- | --- |
| Athens | 655,780 |
| Thessaloníki | 322,240 |
| Patras | 214,580 |
| Iráklion | 173,450 |
| Piraeus | 163,910 |
| Lárissa | 163,380 |

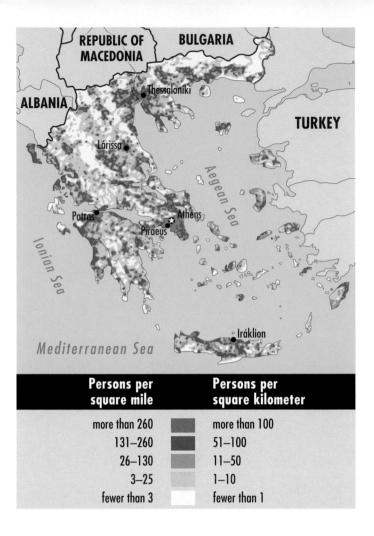

| Persons per square mile | | Persons per square kilometer |
| --- | :---: | --- |
| more than 260 | | more than 100 |
| 131–260 | | 51–100 |
| 26–130 | | 11–50 |
| 3–25 | | 1–10 |
| fewer than 3 | | fewer than 1 |

Albania's government collapsed in 1991, hundreds of thousands of Albanians fled over the border to Greece. Today, Albanians are the country's largest non-Greek population. Other immigrants include Kurdish people who arrived as refugees from Iraq, Turkey, and Iran.

## Finding a Common Language

Greek is Greece's official language, and almost everyone in the country speaks Greek. It took a long time to arrive at a common language, however. In ancient Greece, people in dif-

### Who Lives in Greece?

| | |
| --- | --- |
| Greek | 93.76% |
| Albanian | 4.32% |
| Bulgarian | 0.39% |
| Romanian | 0.23% |
| Other | 1.30% |

ferent regions spoke different dialects. For example, people in Athens spoke Attic, those in parts of the Peloponnese spoke Doric, and many island residents spoke Ionic. Attic became the major language of the golden age. This dialect is also known as Hellenistic Greek or the Alexandrian dialect.

After the conquests of Alexander the Great, the Attic dialect spread throughout the empire. It became the common language for business and learning. Along the way, borrowed words and phrases from other peoples got mixed

An immigrant girl carries food from a charity home to her family in a poor section of Athens. In recent years, many immigrants from eastern Europe and western Asia have come to Greece.

**The airport in Athens has signs in both Greek and English.**

in. This mixed version of Greek was called Koine. Under the Byzantine Empire, Koine became the official language of the government and the Orthodox Church. Meanwhile, ordinary people spoke a common language that evolved from ancient Greek, called *dimotiki*, or demotic.

During the independence movement, some Greek scholars wanted to "purify" the language. They removed all foreign words to create an artificial form of Greek called Katharevousa. This became the official language of the new nation. Few people could master both demotic and the new dialect, and schoolchildren had an especially hard time. By 1976, Katharevousa had lost its appeal, and demotic Greek became Greece's official language. Modern Greek today includes words and expressions borrowed from English, French, Italian, Slavic, Turkish, and Katharevousa.

People in certain regions speak local versions of Greek. Some of these dialects are Cretan in Crete, Maniot in the Máni Peninsula of the Peloponnese, Pontic in the Macedonia region, Sarakatsani in the mountains of northern and central Greece, and Tsakonian in the eastern Peloponnese. Among the Muslim minority in Thrace, Turkish, Bulgarian, and Romany are spoken.

## The Greek Alphabet

Take a look at street signs in Greece, and you may see two different sets of directions. One is in a form you probably can't

### From the Greek

You are more familiar with the Greek language than you think. Thousands of English words came from Greek. In some cases, the Romans adapted a Greek word into Latin before it made its way into English.

| English | Greek Origin |
|---|---|
| academy | *Akademeia* (the school where Plato taught) |
| acrobat | *akrobatos* (walking up high) |
| cosmetics | *kosmetikos* (skilled in adornment) |
| dynamic | *dynamikos* (powerful) |
| echo | *eche* (sound) |
| electronic | *elektron,* from *elektor* (beaming sun) |
| fantastic | *phantastikos* (producing mental images) |
| idea | *eidenai* (to know), *idein* (to see) |
| logical | *logos* (reason) |
| melody | *meloidia* (chanting, music) |
| mystery | *mysterion,* from *mystos* (keeping silence) |
| myth | *mythos* (myth) |
| philosophy | *philos* (beloved) + *sophia* (wisdom) |
| politics | *politikos* (political), *polites* (citizen) |
| zoo | *zoe* (life) |

**Common Greek Words and Phrases**

| | |
|---|---|
| *yia sou (YAH soo)* | hello/good-bye (informal) |
| *yia sas (YAH sahs)* | hello/good-bye (formal) |
| *Ti kanis? (tee KAH-nees)* | How are you? (informal) |
| *Ti kanete? (tee KAH-neh-teh)* | How are you? (formal) |
| *Ime kala. (ee-MEH kah-LAH)* | I'm fine. |
| *parakalo (pah-rah-kah-LOH)* | please |
| *efharisto (eff-hah-ree-STOH)* | thank you |
| *ne (NEH)* | yes |
| *ohi (OH-hee)* | no |

understand. The other is written in letters you can read. That is because the Greek language can be written in the Greek alphabet or the Latin alphabet.

Greek writers were using the Greek alphabet as early as the 700s BCE. It consists of twenty-four characters, from *alpha* to *omega*. With some changes along the way, the Modern Greek alphabet evolved directly from the alphabet used in ancient Greece. The Greek alphabet has many offshoots. It is the ancestor of the Cyrillic script, used in Russian and other Slavic languages. It is also the basis of the Latin alphabet. The words you are reading on this page use the Latin alphabet.

Mathematics and other sciences use Greek letters to stand for certain concepts. For example, one letter of the Greek alphabet is *pi* ($\pi$). In math, pi is used to represent the ratio of a circle's circumference (the length around the circle) to its diameter (the length across the circle). Another Greek letter is *delta* ($\Delta$). The word *delta* refers to the triangular pattern of streams at a river's mouth.

## Learning and Literacy

For you, a gymnasium is a place for exercise and sports. For the ancient Greeks, a gymnasium was a place where athletes trained for competitions. Today, *gymnasio* (gymnasium) is the term for Greece's middle schools, or lower secondary schools.

Children in Greece must attend school between the ages of six and fifteen. One to two years of kindergarten is encouraged but not required. Primary school (*dimotiko*) lasts for six years, from ages six through twelve. Then students spend three

Greek schoolchildren visit a museum in Athens.

# The Greek Alphabet

| Greek Letter Upper Case | Greek Letter Lower Case | Name | English Equivalent | Sound |
|---|---|---|---|---|
| A | α | alpha | a | as in *father* |
| B | β | beta | b | |
| Γ | γ | gamma | g | |
| Δ | δ | delta | d | |
| E | ε | epsilon | e | as in *end* |
| Z | ζ | zeta | z | |
| H | η | eta | e | as in *hey* |
| Θ | θ | theta | th | as in *thick* |
| I | ι | iota | i | as in *it* |
| K | κ | kappa | k | |
| Λ | λ | lambda | l | |
| M | μ | mu | m | |
| N | ν | nu | n | |
| Ξ | ξ | xi | ks | as in *box* |
| O | ο | omicron | o | as in *off* |
| Π | π | pi | p | |
| P | ρ | rho | r | |
| Σ | σ, ς | sigma | s | |
| T | τ | tau | t | |
| Υ | υ | upsilon | u | as in *put* |
| Φ | φ | phi | f | |
| X | χ | chi | ch | as in *Bach* |
| Ψ | ψ | psi | ps | |
| Ω | ω | omega | o | as in *grow* |

years in gymnasio, from ages twelve to fifteen. After gymnasio, students can stop their schooling altogether. For those who continue, students on an academic track may go on to three years of upper secondary school (*lykeio*). Others may take vocational training to prepare for a career.

A student works on a marble sculpture at an art school in Tínos.

For higher education, students can choose a university, a technological educational institute (TEI), or a specialized academy. Greece has about two dozen universities. The largest are the Aristotle University of Thessaloníki and the National and Kapodistrian University of Athens. Courses in TEIs may range from electronics to graphic arts to nursing to shipbuilding. Academies provide military, naval, police, and firefighter training.

Many young people go out of the country for their higher education. That is partly because Greek universities get many more applicants than they can accept. Another reason is that many Greek universities are not able to buy the most up-to-date teaching equipment.

# A Spiritual Land

FREEDOM OF RELIGION IS GUARANTEED IN GREECE'S constitution. However, church and state are more connected in Greece than in many other democratic countries.

The Greek Orthodox Church is the nation's official religion, and many religious holidays are also national holidays. Proselytizing, or trying to convert others to one's own religion, is outlawed. Greece is the only EU country with such a ban. The government pays priests' salaries and education expenses and pays for church repairs. When a new prime minister is sworn in, the head of the Greek Orthodox Church presides over the ceremony. Historians point out that this church–state bond grew out of Greece's four hundred years under Ottoman rule. People kept their sense of Greek identity alive by holding on to their faith.

Muslims are Greece's largest religious minority. Most are ethnic Turks who live in western Thrace and the Dodecanese

*Opposite:* **Monks form a procession at a monastery on Mount Athos. Twenty monasteries are located on this mountain in northeastern Greece.**

| Religion in Greece | |
|---|---|
| Greek Orthodox | 98% |
| Muslim | 1.3% |
| Other | 0.7% |

islands. Small communities of Roman Catholics, Jehovah's Witnesses, Protestants, and Jews also live in Greece.

## Europe's First Christians

Greece was a hotbed of early Christianity. In fact, Greece was the first place in Europe where St. Paul preached Christianity. He set up Europe's first Christian community in Philippi and then moved on to Thessaloníki. In Athens, Paul preached from atop the Areopagus—the massive stone at the base of

St. Paul brought Christianity to Greece. He is shown preaching at Athens in this painting by Raphael, a great Italian Renaissance artist.

the Acropolis. Then he went to Corinth for a year and a half. Other trips took him to the Aegean Islands, as well as Ephesus, a Greek city on the Turkish coast. After he left he wrote epistles, or letters, to the Greek Christian communities of the Philippians, Thessalonians, Corinthians, and Ephesians.

Christianity continued to grow in Greece and other Mediterranean lands. By the 300s CE, Christianity had five major centers, each headed by a patriarch. The patriarchs of Rome and Constantinople had an uneasy relationship, for each one believed he was Christianity's principal leader.

Eastern and Western Christianity split apart in 1054. During the Byzantine and Ottoman eras, the Greek Orthodox Church was under the rule of the patriarch of Constantinople. The church of Greece became independent from Constantinople in 1850.

**The Church of One Hundred Doors on the island of Páros is the oldest remaining Byzantine church in Greece. Parts of it date back to 328 CE.**

Today, Greek Orthodoxy is self-governing—that is, it is not subject to a higher authority. Its head is the archbishop of Athens, also called the primate of Greece. Some parts of Greece remain subject to the patriarch of Constantinople. They include northern Greece, Mount Athos, Crete, and the Dodecanese Islands.

## Metropolitans, Priests, and Monks

The archbishop of Athens presides over a synod of metropolitans, or council of bishops. The synod makes decisions about issues that arise in the church. The archdiocese of Athens is divided into eighty-one dioceses, with a metropolitan overseeing each one. Thirty-six of those dioceses, however, are under the patriarch of Constantinople.

Only men can become priests. To become a priest, a young man studies theology for at least two years. Those who hope to be a bishop one day take further studies at the universities of Athens or Thessaloníki. Greek Orthodox priests may marry, but only before they have taken their final vows. Only unmarried priests can become metropolitans. Priests' salaries are rather low, so many priests take second jobs. Priests wear a long, black robe; a round, high hat; long hair; and a beard.

Monks are priests who belong to a monastery, or religious community. They take vows of poverty, chastity, and obedience. In the more conservative monasteries, daily life is a combination of prayer, fasting, and rigorous discipline. Because monks don't marry, most of the church's metropolitans are monks. Some monasteries house communities

of women dedicated to a spiritual life. Many of them operate schools, orphanages, and medical centers.

Orthodox priests wear elaborate gold robes in religious festivals.

## Historic Monasteries

Greece has more than two hundred monasteries, and some are more than a thousand years old. Countless monasteries were founded during the Byzantine period. They featured several buildings, often including a bakery, an oil press, and a library. Many monks were scholars who translated ancient Greek works into the Byzantine dialect.

Greece's most famous monasteries are Mount Athos and Metéora. Mount Athos, also called the Holy Mountain, includes a group of twenty monasteries. Monks first settled there in the 700s CE, and the complex now houses beautiful paintings, icons, and manuscripts. Close to two thousand monks live there today. Some are hard at work restoring and cataloging the monastery's many precious art objects. Only men can visit Mount Athos, and only if they get permission from the site in advance.

An awesome sight greets visitors to western Thessaly. Twenty-four towering pillars of sandstone rock rise straight up above the plains. Scientists believe they were formed 60 million years ago, and earthquakes and erosion shaped them into spires. Perched high on the rocks' craggy peaks are a group of

**Orthodox priests usually wear long black robes.**

monasteries. Monks began living there in the 800s CE. They named their community Metéora, meaning "suspended in the air." Twenty-four monasteries flourished at Metéora in the 1500s, but only six remain today, including two for women.

Mount Athos is located near the coast of the Aegean Sea. Most visitors arrive by boat and then catch a bus or taxi up the rough, unpaved roads to the monasteries.

## Beliefs and Practices

The Greek Orthodox Church is one of several Eastern Orthodox churches. They all share the same basic beliefs and traditions. Like other Eastern Orthodox faiths, Greek Orthodoxy claims an unbroken line of bishops from the time of the apostles, the first people to spread the news of Jesus, until today. Church services

## The Original Icons

Greek Orthodox churches are richly adorned with icons. These are gold-highlighted paintings of Jesus; Mary, his mother; or saints. Icons are also used in homes and shrines.

Traditional icon subjects are the Preparation—an empty throne awaiting Christ's return—and the Dormition—Mary's ascent into heaven. Favorite saints include St. George, St. Andrew of Patras, St. Demetrios of Thessaloníki, St. Michael, St. Nicholas, St. John the Baptist, and the Three Hierarchs—Sts. John Chrysostom, Basil, and Gregory.

The word *icon* comes from the Greek word meaning "image." Today, the word *iconoclast* means someone who attacks established beliefs or institutions. The term originated in the 700s CE, when Byzantine emperor Leo III introduced a policy of iconoclasm ("the breaking of icons"). He charged that using icons was worshipping idols and ordered them all to be destroyed. The policy was ended a century later.

use the Greek Koine language of the Byzantine period and follow the Byzantine rite, an ancient set of ceremonies rich with symbolism. Services include incense burning and chanting. The typical Greek Orthodox church is built in the Byzantine style. It is designed in the shape of a Greek cross, with four equal-sized arms. Over the center rises a massive dome, symbolizing the vault of heaven, with a cross on top.

When babies are baptized, they are dipped in water three times. In weddings, the bride and groom are crowned with white wreaths joined by a ribbon.

Religious festivals are an important part of Greek culture. Besides attending church services, people celebrate by feasting, singing, and dancing. Easter is the most important holiday of the year. The Christmas season has many occasions for celebration, including Christmas itself, St. Basil's Day on January 1, and Epiphany on January 6. People also celebrate important saints' days and the feasts of village patron saints.

**A procession of icons is part of the celebration of Easter Week on the island of Kárpathos.**

# Culture
# and Fun

G O TO ANY WEDDING, FESTIVAL, OR BIRTHDAY party in Greece, and people are likely to break out in a traditional Greek dance. Forming a circle or a long line, they link their arms across one another's shoulders and begin lively footwork. For traditional Greek folk dancers, costumes often consist of wide-sleeved white shirts and high black boots for men and headscarves and colorful aprons for women.

## Diverse Dances

Each region has its own dance style, but Greek people all over the world love to dance the *kalamatianos*. The main dancer leads the second dancer as they hold either end of a handkerchief. This dance may have originated in the olive-growing Kalamáta region in southern Greece. To celebrate a rich harvest, women used to take off their scarves and wave them as they whirled around in a circle.

**Dancing is part of many events in Greece.**

The *zalongo* dance recalls the tragic story of the brave Souliot women. Fleeing Turkish forces, the women of Souli, in northwestern Greece, danced up onto a cliff. Then they flung themselves and their children over the edge to avoid being captured. The *tsamikos* is slow and stately, but it involves high jumps and kicks. Each dancer in the row performs athletic, leaping footwork, trying to outdo the previous dancer.

Only one person at a time dances the *zeibekiko*. The dancer makes up the steps, sometimes dancing in a circle around a glass of wine or a chair. The *hassapiko* has both a slow version and a fast version. It began in the Middle Ages as a dance imitating swordplay in battle. Out of the hassapiko grew the *syrtaki* dance, made popular in the movie *Zorba the Greek*. The *pentozali*, a war dance as well as a folk dance, began on the island of Crete. It involves vigorous high jumps and gets faster and faster.

## Folk, Pop, and Classical Music

Some early Greek folk instruments were shepherds' flutes made from reeds, wood, or animal bones. Goatherds would join in, playing harmony with bells hanging from their goats' necks. This gentle image is a far cry from today's popular Greek music, though. Now even traditional instruments are electrified and amplified.

For folk music and dance, the bouzouki is the main instrument. It's like a fat-bodied guitar. Another folk instrument is a three-stringed lyre played with a bow. The *zourna*, a type of oboe, used to give folk music its sharp, piercing melody lines. Now, most folk bands use a clarinet instead. The *sandouri* is a rectangular instrument that lies flat as the player strikes its strings with sticks.

*Rebetiko* songs in Greece are like the blues in the United States. They're songs of the urban poor. Since the mid-twentieth century, *laïkó* was the mainstream popular music. Then musicians began to mix laïkó with modern pop and rock elements, creating today's *laïkó-pop*. Fans enjoy laïkó-pop in nightclubs called *bouzoukia*, where they compliment the performers by throwing flowers and napkins onstage.

Greek composer Mikis Theodorakis is known worldwide, especially for writing the music for the movies *Zorba the Greek*, *Z*, and *Serpico*. Modern composer Evangelos Odysseas Papathanassiou goes by the stage name Vangelis. His music for the movie *Chariots of Fire* won an Academy Award. Vangelis also wrote the scores for the movies *Blade Runner*; *1492: Conquest of Paradise*; and *Alexander*. Composer Iannis Xenakis was born in

Romania to Greek parents. Using mathematics as a basis for his music, he was a pioneer in developing electronic music.

Dimitri Mitropoulos of Athens became the conductor of the Minneapolis Symphony Orchestra, the New York Philharmonic, and New York's Metropolitan Opera. Famous for his excellent memory, Mitropoulos conducted without looking at a musical score.

## Celebrating Greek Culture

Hardly a day goes by in Greece without some kind of festival going on. Some festivals are unique to one city or region, while others are celebrated nationwide.

Conductor Dimitri Mitropoulos was a great supporter of modern classical music.

## The National Archaeological Museum

Many of the best finds from Greece's archaeological digs end up in the National Archaeological Museum in Athens. This is one of the richest archaeological museums in the world. Its collections represent every culture that flourished in Greece since the 6000s BCE. One of the museum's most famous items is the gold-covered Mask of Agamemnon (left), from the ruins of Mycenae. There are marble sculptures and statues from ancient gravesites and temples, as well as bronze horsemen, warriors, and gods. The museum also houses a collection of ancient Egyptian art.

The Athens and Epidaurus Festival lights up the warm summer nights in these two cities. Festival shows run from May through October every year. The major venue is the outdoor Odeon of Herodes Atticus, at the foot of the Acropolis. A rich man named Herodes built this stone amphitheater in 161 CE, in memory of his deceased wife. Musicians, actors, poets, and dancers used to perform there to win the favor of the gods. Now the festival features orchestras, operas, and dance concerts.

Many other festivals take place on the Peloponnese. On the tip of the Peloponnese, the seaside city of Náfplio holds an international festival of classical music every June. Kalamáta presents the Kalamáta International Dance Festival every July. And from July to August, the Ancient Olympia Festival and Ancient Ilida Festival offer Greek tragedies and comedies, concerts, and exhibitions.

Greece has more archaeological museums than anywhere else in the world. Many ancient sites have their own museum of excavated treasures, ranging from statues and pieces of architecture to jewelry, dinnerware, and personal items. Corinth, Epidaurus, Olympia, Delphi, Pella, Philippi, Rhodes, Santorini, the Acropolis, and many other places have on-site museums. Crete's Heraklion Archaeological Museum has the world's biggest collection of artifacts from the Minoan civilization. Some of the best ancient finds, however, now rest in Athens's National Archaeological Museum.

Dozens of museums throughout the country display Byzantine art. The largest is the Byzantine and Christian Museum in Athens, featuring Byzantine icons, illuminated manuscripts, and ceremonial objects encrusted with precious stones. Many monasteries, too, have their own museums of Byzantine treasures.

### El Greco

One of Greece's most famous artists was Doménikos Theotokópoulos (1541–1614). Few people recognize that name, though. He is better known as El Greco ("The Greek"), the nickname he was given in Spain. El Greco was born in Crete and eventually settled in Toledo, Spain. He is best known for dramatic paintings of religious subjects. His figures have long bodies that look stretched from top to bottom, and his skies are often dark or have an eerie glow.

Ancient Greece's most famous writers were the philosophers Plato (ca. 428–ca. 348 BCE) and his student Aristotle (384–322 BCE). They laid the foundations for logical thinking and mathematics in the Western world. Greece's greatest storyteller was the poet Homer, who lived around the eighth century BCE. Stories from his two epic poems are still being retold today. One is *The Iliad*, about the mythological warrior Achilles and the Trojan War. The other is *The Odyssey*, recounting the heroic adventures of the voyager Odysseus.

Aesop was another Greek writer of ancient times. Allegedly, he was a storyteller of the sixth century BCE. But scholars are not sure whether he was a mythological character himself! He is credited with the group of moral tales known as *Aesop's Fables*. "The Tortoise and the Hare," "The Ant and the Grasshopper," and "The Fox and the Grapes" are some of these beloved fables.

In modern times, Níkos Kazantzákis is Greece's most renowned writer. Born in Crete, he glorified the hearty, heroic nature of Cretans. His best-known novels, *Zorba the Greek*

Little is known of the ancient Greek poet Homer. Experts assume he came from a region known as Ionia, along the central Aegean coast, because of the version of the Greek language used in his works.

Greek athletes carry a giant Greek flag during the opening ceremony of the Olympic Games in Athens in 2004.

and *The Last Temptation of Christ*, were both made into movies. Two Greek poets have won the Nobel Prize in Literature: George Seferis (1963) and Odysseus Elytis (1979).

### The Olympics—Welcome Home!

Ancient Greece was the birthplace of the most famous sports event in the world. Olympia held the world's first Olympic games in 776 BCE. With only a few exceptions, they took place every four years for almost 1,200 years. The ancient games ended around 400 CE. Then, almost 1,500 years later, the Olympics were born again—in Greece. The first modern Olympic Games took place in Athens in 1896. Only fourteen countries and 241 athletes participated.

More than a century passed before the Olympics returned to their birthplace. Athens hosted the 2004 Summer Olympic Games, taking the motto Welcome Home! The city flew into a frenzy of preparations, expanding its Olympic Sports Complex, extending roads and rail lines, and building a new international airport to handle the influx of people. The Olympics were a great success. To top it off, Greek athletes proudly walked away with sixteen medals.

### Soccer and Other Sports

Greek kids and adults alike are wild about soccer, also known as football. A pickup game is likely to start on any street corner or vacant lot. Fans are fiercely loyal to their favorite local, regional, and national clubs. Greece's national team won the European Football Championship (UEFA) in 2004. The team also made it to the 2010 World Cup but lost to Argentina in the finals.

Basketball and volleyball are also popular throughout the country. In 2011, Greece's national basketball team ranked fourth in the world in the International Basketball Federation (FIBA) lineup. Olympiakos, the top volleyball team, is one of the best in Europe. Greek athletes have been world champions in Greco-Roman wrestling, weight lifting, track and field, water polo, sailing, and rowing.

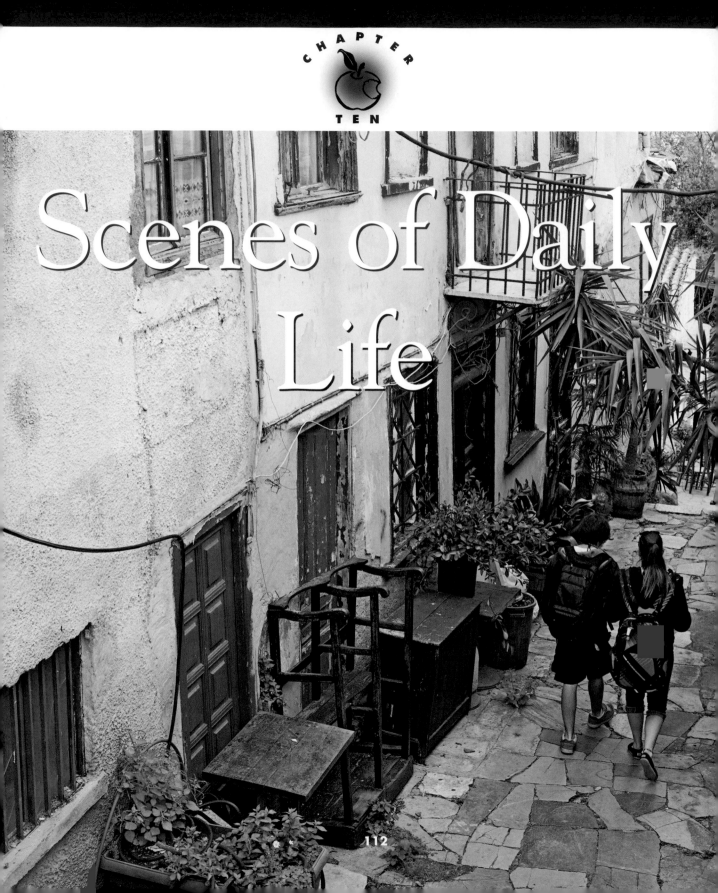

# Scenes of Daily Life

THROUGH THE YEARS, MORE AND MORE GREEK PEOPLE have left their rural farms and moved to the cities. Today, most Greeks live in urban areas. Streets are jam-packed with traffic zooming past modern apartments, office buildings, movie theaters, fast-food restaurants, and shopping centers. Here and there, jugglers, musicians, acrobats, and other street performers show off their talents to entertain the passersby. City nights are late nights. Dinner is rarely served before 9:00 or 10:00 at night, and many people eat after 11:00. Then they meet with friends and go to music shows, bars, or discos until the wee hours.

A sense of history is never far away in Greece. Most Greek cities have a historic quarter, where old homes and shops line the narrow alleys, laundry flutters on clotheslines overhead, and the smells of delicious food drift through the air.

Some common problems come with the growing city populations. In Athens, even with its many high-rise apartment buildings, there is barely enough housing to hold the constant

*Opposite:* **Steep, narrow streets cut through the old part of Athens.**

**Cars clog the streets of Athens during rush hour.**

influx of new arrivals. Traffic jams are common, and exhaust from the thousands of vehicles creates serious air pollution problems. That pollution, unfortunately, stains and decays the area's ancient monuments.

## Village Life

Farming is so hard in Greece's mountainous areas that many mountain dwellers have abandoned their farms. But family farming still flourishes on the rich plains of the central region and the coast. Most farmhouses have heat and electricity. They are typically covered in stucco (a mixture of cement, sand, water, and lime) and have red tile roofs. In the yard, there are often flower and vegetable gardens, a chicken coop, a donkey, and a couple of goats.

For farm families, much of the day is spent outdoors, and the seasons and times of day rule their daily activities. Both kids and adults help with the chores. Cattle, sheep, and goats must be fed, fruit trees must be pruned, and wheat and other crops must be planted and harvested.

Not everyone who lives in rural Greece is a farmer. All villages need bakeries, taverns, restaurants, grocery stores, and other small businesses. Like kids almost everywhere, Greece's farm kids and shopkeepers' kids spend a lot of time using their cell phones, but they also roam the poppy-covered fields, take their dogs on long walks, and enjoy the clean air.

## Family Life

Family ties in Greece are strong, loving, and caring. Parents consider it a serious duty to give their children a good education. Even in hard times, parents spend as much money as possible to feed, clothe, and educate their children. At the same time, discipline tends to be strict. When children are grown up, parents often help them out financially.

Elderly people are highly respected in Greece. Friends and relatives seek them out for their wisdom, and their advice is prized. The elderly are addressed with courtesy and served first at mealtimes. Older people often live with their children, but if they live in a home for the elderly, their children visit frequently.

Social life occurs outdoors in the hot summer months. Once the blazing sun drops, people enjoy strolling up and down the main street or along the seaside. But cafés and coffeehouses are popular any time of year. Lounging around the *kafenion*, or Greek coffeehouse, is a long-standing village tradition. The kafenion used to be strictly male territory. Men would gather there for hours to talk about work, politics, the latest news, and the changing society. A pack of cards or a *tavli* (backgammon) game was standard equipment. Now, both

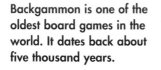

Backgammon is one of the oldest board games in the world. It dates back about five thousand years.

## Playing Berlina

Berlina is a traditional children's game in Greece. A small group of children can play it. First, one child is chosen to be Berlina, and another child is chosen to be the leader. Each child whispers an unusual fact about Berlina to the leader. The facts are bits of information such as Berlina has a spotted dog, Berlina loves to dance, Berlina likes a certain book, Berlina has a crush on Nikos, and so on. Then the leader recites the facts to Berlina without revealing who said them. Berlina tries to guess who is the source of each fact. The first child whose name Berlina guesses correctly becomes Berlina in the next game.

men and women might be seen in a kafenion, although old men are still the most common patrons.

As city jobs have become harder to find, some city dwellers are moving back to the villages where their parents or grandparents grew up. They apply their business and technical skills to traditional rural occupations. Some make part of their farmhouse into a bed-and-breakfast. Others take in tourists who want to spend their vacations working on a farm. In a fast-moving world, these former city folk enjoy slowing down and getting in touch with their rural roots.

### The Joys of Greek Food

Greeks have what is called a Mediterranean diet. Their meals are a bountiful mix of fresh foods straight from the farm: tomatoes, onions, garlic, olives, eggplant, fruit, and fresh-baked bread. Dairy products such as goat cheese and yogurt are included in most meals. Meat dishes usually feature lamb, but chicken, beef, pork, and seafood are also available fresh. Meat and vegetables are often combined to make thick stews. Fresh fish such as swordfish, sole, mackerel, and sardines are

## Let's Make Tirópita!

Tirópita, or cheese pie, is a popular Greek food. People might eat tirópita for breakfast or as a mid-morning or mid-afternoon snack between meals.

### Ingredients

10 sheets phyllo pastry dough

2 cups ricotta cheese

5 ounces feta cheese

2 eggs

1 teaspoon cinnamon

1 cup milk

2 tablespoons melted butter

### Directions

Preheat the oven to 350°F. Unfold the phyllo dough and set it out to dry. Crumble the cheeses in a large mixing bowl. In a separate bowl, beat the eggs and add the cinnamon and milk. Add this mixture to the cheeses, and mix it together. Butter a medium-sized baking pan. Place one sheet of phyllo dough in the bottom of the pan and spread melted butter on it. Add four more layers of phyllo dough with butter. Spread the mixture on top of the phyllo layers, and smooth out the top so it's level. Add five more sheets of phyllo dough with butter to the top of the cheese mixture. Bake for about 40 minutes, until golden brown. Cut into rectangles to serve. Enjoy!

plentiful, and so are octopus, squid, shrimp, and mussels. One delicious fish specialty is *taramosaláta*, a pinkish-orange puree of fish eggs.

Feta, the national cheese, is made from goat milk. Crumbly, white, and salty, it's an essential ingredient in salads. Traditional Greek salads have no lettuce. Instead, they're made of tomatoes, cucumbers, onions, feta, and olives. Typical Greek bread comes in big, round loaves. Pita is a round flatbread. With a helping of meat and vegetables in the center, it can be rolled up to make a tube-shaped sandwich. If pita is cut in half, each half becomes a pocket for sandwich fillings.

Souvlaki is sometimes cooked on skewers.

Souvlaki sandwiches are as popular and convenient in Greece as hamburgers are in the United States. At souvlaki shops, a vertical piece of meat rotates on a rotisserie. The cook slices off strips of meat into a pita and adds tomatoes, onions, and *tzatzíki*, a yogurt sauce with cucumbers and garlic. Souvlaki is sometimes served as a kebab—chunks of meat, tomatoes, and onions on a skewer. Greeks prepare many delicious casserole dishes, too. One is moussaka, made of ground meat, eggplant, potatoes, and onions baked with a creamy sauce. Another is pastitsio, which is layered noodles, meat, and tomato sauce.

**Pastries drizzled with honey are a delicious treat in Greece.**

## Getting Married

In the most traditional Greek Orthodox weddings, the groom comes to the bride's house on the wedding day and formally asks her father for her hand in marriage. Then the best man escorts the bride and groom to the church. Today, more commonly, the groom arrives at the church first, where he and the guests wait for the bride.

A priest presides over the centuries-old ceremony, which is rich with symbolism. First comes the Service of Betrothal, in which the bride and groom exchange rings, switching them back and forth three times. Then comes the Sacrament of Marriage, with the priest leading the couple in prayers. For the Crowning, the best man places gold crowns or orange-blossom wreaths, connected by a white silk ribbon, on the bride's and groom's heads. This signifies that they are joined as a new family in the sight of God. Next, the priest reads the Bible story of the wedding feast at Cana. Then the couple sips three times from a common cup of wine. This shows they share the burdens and joys of their new life together. Finally, the priest leads the couple in a ceremonial walk around the altar three times.

After the ceremony comes a lavish wedding party that can last for hours, stretching into the night. As party favors, guests receive candy-coated almonds. They consume huge amounts of traditional food and drink, and everyone joins in energetic Greek dances.

Dessert is often fresh fruit such as strawberries, watermelon, oranges, grapes, cherries, peaches, or figs. To satisfy a sweet tooth, people might drop by a pastry shop for sweets and coffee. Typically, cakes and pastries are dripping with honey syrup.

Baklava is a flaky pastry with walnuts or almonds and cinnamon. *Kadaïfi* are threadlike pastry rolls filled with nuts. Greek coffee—thick, strong, and richly flavored—is served in tiny cups. The coffee grounds sink to the bottom of the cup, and a creamy foam rests on top.

## Daily Meals

A Greek breakfast is simple. It may consist only of strong coffee, with maybe a piece of *tirópita* (cheese pie) or a sesame seed bagel. Some people don't eat breakfast. Instead, they wait until mid-morning, when they have tirópita or some other light snack. Lunch, too, is light, and people often stop by cafés or street stalls for lunchtime snacks. They might order tirópita, spanakopita (spinach pie), fried cheese, a souvlaki sandwich, or grape leaves stuffed with rice and onions.

The late evening meal is the high point of the day. For people eating out in a café, or taverna, dinner is served at big tables where diners help themselves to huge platters of food. For Sunday dinners at home, a traditional dish is marinated beef filet. It's usually served with rice dressed up with raisins, apricots, or cherries.

## Festivals and Holidays

Most holidays in Greece are religious holidays, and people celebrate them all over the country. These warm and festive times are a chance for extended families and old friends to reunite. Family ties are strengthened and community bonds are renewed.

Easter is the most important religious feast of the year, but festivities begin weeks before that. First comes three weeks of Apokries, or Carnival season—the Greek version of Mardi Gras. It usually begins in February. To celebrate Apokries, people dress in fancy costumes, take part in parades, throw confetti, and eat, drink, and dance. The most spectacular festivities take place in Patras. Apokries lasts until Kathari

The Patras Carnival features parades with giant floats.

Deftera, or Clean Monday, which begins Lent—the seven weeks before Easter. Traditionally, families spend Clean Monday picnicking and flying kites from hilltops. The next day, Lent begins in earnest as people begin fasting, or going without certain foods.

Easter celebrations begin on Good Friday, a day of mourning commemorating Jesus's death. That night, a priest removes from the church the Epitaphios, a flower-covered shrine, and carries it through the streets. This shrine represents Jesus's tomb. People follow in silence, each one holding a lighted candle, in a funeral procession for Jesus.

## Public Holidays

| | |
|---|---|
| January 1 | New Year's Day |
| January 6 | Feast of Theophany |
| Date varies | Clean Monday |
| March 25 | Independence Day |
| Date varies | Good Friday |
| Date varies | Easter Monday |
| May 1 | Labor Day |
| Date varies | Whit Monday |
| August 15 | Assumption |
| October 28 | *Ochi* Day |
| December 25 | Christmas |
| December 26 | Day after Christmas |

The next night, everyone gathers in church for the Easter Vigil. On the stroke of midnight, the priest announces that Jesus is risen, and people light candles from one person to another. Church bells ring, and fireworks explode in the night sky. Once they are back at home, people eat *magiritsa* soup to break their pre-Easter fast.

For the traditional Easter Sunday dinner, families feast on lamb roasted on a spit. Following a folk custom, each person holds a red-dyed Easter egg and knocks it against the other people's eggs. The person whose egg doesn't crack will have good luck for a whole year.

In Greece, August 15 is a holiday almost as important as Easter. It is the Feast of the Assumption, or the Dormition, celebrating Mary's being taken up into heaven. Many Greeks go back to their hometowns for the celebration. The largest

Holding lit candles is part of the Easter celebration in Greece.

observance takes place at the Church of Panayia Evangelistria on the island of Tínos. Its icon of Mary is believed to have miraculous powers. Thousands of pilgrims, along with many church and secular leaders, come to make offerings, attend the church services, and join in processions.

Greeks also celebrate two patriotic holidays. One is Independence Day, on March 25. It celebrates the beginning of the war of independence against the Ottoman Empire in 1821. The other is Ochi Day, on October 28. "*Ochi!*" (also spelled "*ohi*") means "No!" That's what statesman Ioannis Metaxas said in 1940 when Italy asked if it could move in

**Fireworks light up Syntagma Square in Athens at the opening of the Christmas season.**

troops to occupy parts of Greece. That "no" brought on an invasion by Italy, dragging Greece into World War II. Independence Day and Ochi Day both feature parades, military shows, flag-waving, and people in traditional costumes.

The winter holiday season begins with the Feast of St. Nicholas, December 6. St. Nicholas is honored as the patron saint of sailors and the protector of all who go to sea. Many boats and ships are decorated with sparkling lights that day.

In Athens, the largest Christmas tree in Europe lights up Syntagma Square. Nearby is a Christmas village, complete with elf cottages that sell candy and ornaments. Clowns and other street performers roam around spreading merriment. On Christmas Eve, children go from house to house caroling, and the listeners reward them with money or sweet treats. Only children receive gifts on Christmas Eve.

After church services on Christmas Day comes a huge feast. Roast pork is the traditional main course, although more and more people are now eating a big turkey instead. Favorite sweets include *melomakarona*, which are semolina, cinnamon, and clove cookies drenched in honey. *Christopsomo*, a bread decorated with a cross scored into the top or created with additional dough, is baked on Christmas Eve. On Christmas Day, the head of the family gives a blessing over the bread, and then cuts a piece for each guest.

New Year's Day is also the Feast of St. Basil. Traditionally, a coin is baked into the *Vasilopita* (Basil cake). Whoever gets the slice with the coin will enjoy a year of good luck. St. Basil's Day, rather than Christmas, is the day family and friends give each other gifts. Traditionally, children would leave their shoes by the fireplace in hopes of receiving gifts in them.

The final day of the holiday season is January 6, the Feast of Theophany, known in other countries as the Epiphany. This is the day for the Blessing of the Waters. In Piraeus and other port cities, a priest leads a solemn procession to the waterfront. He blesses the boats assembled there and prays for the sailors' safety. Finally, he tosses a cross into the sea, and boys plunge into the icy waters after it. Whoever finds the cross will be blessed with—what else?—good luck all year long!

# Timeline

| Greek History | | World History |
|---|---|---|
| Minoan civilization flourishes on the island of Crete. | **ca. 2700– 1400** BCE | |
| | **ca. 2500** BCE | Egyptians build the pyramids and the Sphinx in Giza. |
| Mycenaean civilization falls. | **ca. 1100** BCE | |
| The first Olympic games take place at Olympia. | **776** BCE | |
| Athens declares itself a democracy. | **508** BCE | **ca. 563** BCE The Buddha is born in India. |
| Greece's golden age, or Classical period, is at its peak. | **400s** BCE | |
| Alexander the Great dies; Greece's Hellenistic period begins. | **323** BCE | |
| The Roman Empire takes control of Greece. | **146** BCE | |
| The Byzantine period begins. | **330** CE | **313** CE The Roman emperor Constantine legalizes Christianity. |
| | **610** | The Prophet Muhammad begins preaching a new religion called Islam. |
| The Christian Church breaks into Eastern and Western branches. | **1054** | **1054** The Eastern (Orthodox) and Western (Roman Catholic) Churches break apart. |
| | **1095** | The Crusades begin. |
| | **1215** | King John seals the Magna Carta. |
| | **1300s** | The Renaissance begins in Italy. |
| | **1347** | The plague sweeps through Europe. |
| The Byzantine Empire, including Greece, becomes part of the Ottoman Empire. | **1453** | **1453** Ottoman Turks capture Constantinople, conquering the Byzantine Empire. |
| | **1492** | Columbus arrives in North America. |
| | **1500s** | Reformers break away from the Catholic Church, and Protestantism is born. |

## Greek History

| | |
|---|---|
| Greeks begin fighting a war of independence against the Ottomans. | 1821 |
| Greece becomes a constitutional monarchy. | 1844 |
| First modern Olympic Games are held in Athens. | 1896 |
| Greece's "*Ochi!*" ("No!") to Italy's occupation brings Greece into World War II. | 1940 |
| Army officers seize control of the Greek government. | 1967 |
| Democracy is restored; Greece is proclaimed a republic. | 1973 |
| Greece joins the European Economic Community. | 1981 |
| The Summer Olympics are held in Athens. | 2004 |
| High government debts usher in a severe financial crisis. | 2010 |

## World History

| | |
|---|---|
| 1776 | The U.S. Declaration of Independence is signed. |
| 1789 | The French Revolution begins. |
| 1865 | The American Civil War ends. |
| 1879 | The first practical lightbulb is invented. |
| 1914 | World War I begins. |
| 1917 | The Bolshevik Revolution brings communism to Russia. |
| 1929 | A worldwide economic depression begins. |
| 1939 | World War II begins. |
| 1945 | World War II ends. |
| 1957 | The Vietnam War begins. |
| 1969 | Humans land on the Moon. |
| 1975 | The Vietnam War ends. |
| 1989 | The Berlin Wall is torn down as communism crumbles in Eastern Europe. |
| 1991 | The Soviet Union breaks into separate states. |
| 2001 | Terrorists attack the World Trade Center in New York City and the Pentagon near Washington, D.C. |
| 2004 | A tsunami in the Indian Ocean destroys coastlines in Africa, India, and Southeast Asia. |
| 2008 | The United States elects its first African American president. |

# Fast Facts

**Official name:** Hellenic Republic

**Capital:** Athens

**Official language:** Greek

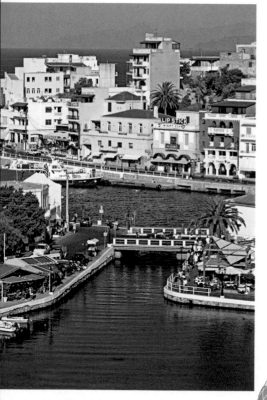

Iráklion

Greek flag

Pindus Mountains

| | |
|---|---|
| **Official religion:** | Greek Orthodox |
| **National anthem:** | "Ýmnos eis tin Eleftherian" ("Ode to Liberty") |
| **Type of government:** | Parliamentary republic |
| **Chief of state:** | President |
| **Head of government:** | Prime minister |
| **Area:** | 50,942 square miles (131,940 sq km) |
| **Bordering countries:** | Albania to the northwest, Bulgaria and the Republic of Macedonia to the north, and Turkey to the east |
| **Highest elevation:** | Mount Olympus, 9,570 feet (2,917 m) above sea level |
| **Lowest elevation:** | Sea level along the coast |
| **Length of coastline:** | 9,333 miles (15,020 km), including the coasts of islands |
| **Number of Islands:** | About 6,000; 227 populated |
| **Average high temperature:** | Athens: 92°F (33°C) in July; 55°F (13°C) in January |
| **Average low temperature:** | Athens: 73°F (23°C) in July; 44°F (7°C) in January |
| **Average annual precipitation:** | Athens: 15 inches (38 cm) |

Patras

National population
(2011 est.): 10,787,690

Population of major
cities (2011 est.):

| | |
|---|---|
| Athens | 655,780 |
| Thessaloníki | 322,240 |
| Patras | 214,580 |
| Iráklion | 173,450 |
| Piraeus | 163,910 |

Landmarks:
- ▶ *Acropolis*, Athens
- ▶ *Knossos palace*, Crete
- ▶ *Metéora*, western Thessaly
- ▶ *National Archaeological Museum*, Athens
- ▶ *Temple of Apollo*, Delphi

Economy: Services, which include tourism, make up the largest segment of the Greek economy. The major manufacturing products are petroleum products, foods, textiles, and cement. Leading agricultural products include corn, olives and olive oil, wheat, and dairy products such as cheese and milk. Greece's mines produce lignite coal, bauxite, and other minerals.

Currency: The euro (€). In 2012, €0.77 was equal to US$1, and €1 was equal to US$1.31.

System of weights
and measures: Metric system

Literacy rate (2011): 97.2%

Currency

Children

Dimitri Mitropoulos

**Common Greek words and phrases:**

| | |
|---|---|
| *yia sou* | hello/good-bye (informal) |
| *yia sas* | hello/good-bye (formal) |
| *Ti kanis?* | How are you? (informal) |
| *Ti kanete?* | How are you? (formal) |
| *Ime kala.* | I'm fine. |
| *parakalo* | please |
| *efharisto* | thank you |
| *ne* | yes |
| *ohi* | no |

**Prominent Greeks:**

Aristotle (384–322 BCE)
*Philosopher*

El Greco (1541–1614)
*Artist*

Euclid (flourished ca. 300 BCE)
*Mathematician known as the Father of Geometry*

Hippocrates (ca. 460–ca. 377 BCE)
*First doctor to use scientific methods*

Ioánnis Kapodístrias (1776–1831)
*First prime minister*

Níkos Kazantzákis (1883–1957)
*Novelist*

Andreas Papandreou (1919–1996)
*Founder of the Panhellenic Socialist Movement (PASOK) party*

Plato (ca. 428–ca. 348 BCE)
*Philosopher*

# To Find Out More

## Books

- Green, Jen. *Greece*. Washington, D.C.: National Geographic Children's Books, 2009.

- Pearson, Anne. *Ancient Greece*. New York: DK Children, 2007.

- Steele, Philip. *Navigators: Ancient Greece*. New York: Macmillan, 2011.

- Villing, Alexandra. *The Ancient Greeks: Their Lives and Their World*. Los Angeles: J. Paul Getty Museum, 2010.

- Wilhelm, Doug. *Alexander the Great: Master of the Ancient World*. New York: Franklin Watts, 2010.

## DVDs

- *Athens: The Dawn of Democracy*. PBS, 2007.

- *Greece: Pyramids and Mummies*. A&E Home Video, 2010.

- *Secrets of the Parthenon*. PBS/Nova, 2008.

- *Women in Ancient Greece*. Gregory Zorzos, 2009.

▶ Visit this Scholastic Web site for more information on Greece:
**www.factsfornow.scholastic.com**
Enter the keyword **Greece**

# Index

Page numbers in *italics* indicate illustrations.

# Meet the Author

Ann Heinrichs begins to get itchy if she hasn't been out of the country for a while. She has traveled through much of Europe, as well as the Middle East, East Asia, and Africa. In Greece, she explored ancient archaeological sites, trekked through the countryside, scrambled across the islands, and devoured lots of delicious Greek food.

Heinrichs grew up roaming the woods of Arkansas. Now she lives in Chicago, Illinois. She has written more than two hundred books for children and young adults on American, European, Asian, and African history and culture. Some of her other titles in the Enchantment of the World series are *Brazil, Japan, Egypt, Niger, Nigeria, Ethopia,* and *Wales.* Several of her books have won state and national awards.

"When I'm starting a country book," says Heinrichs, "I head for the library's reference department. Some of my favorite resources are United Nations publications, *Europa World Year Book,* and the periodicals databases. For this book, I also read online issues of *Athens News* and other newspapers to get a feel for Greeks' current interests and viewpoints. I have

some Greek friends, too, so I interviewed them about Greek food, family, and customs."

Heinrichs has also written many newspaper, magazine, and encyclopedia articles. As an advertising copywriter, she has covered everything from plumbing hardware to Oriental rugs. She holds bachelor's and master's degrees in piano performance and, most recently, a master of library and information science (MLIS) degree. For fun, she enjoys bicycling along Chicago's lakefront and kayaking.

# Photo Credits